27 SEPTEMBER,
1985

PALO

D0622745

New Perspectives on the South
Charles P. Roland, General Editor

The Self-Inflicted Wound

❧

Southern Politics in the Nineteenth Century

ROBERT F. DURDEN

THE UNIVERSITY PRESS OF KENTUCKY

Copyright © 1985 by The University Press of Kentucky

Scholarly publisher for the Commonwealth,
serving Bellarmine College, Berea College, Centre
College of Kentucky, Eastern Kentucky University,
The Filson Club, Georgetown College, Kentucky
Historical Society, Kentucky State University,
Northern Kentucky University, Transylvania University,
University of Kentucky, University of Louisville,
and Western Kentucky University.

Editorial and Sales Offices: Lexington, Kentucky 40506-0024

Library of Congress Cataloging in Publication Data

Durden, Robert Franklin.
    The self-inflicted wound.

    (New perspectives on the South)
    Bibliography: p.
    Includes index.
    1. Southern States—Politics and government—1775–1865.
2. Southern States—Politics and government—1865–1950.
I. Title. II. Series.
F213.D87   1985   975   84-29173
ISBN 0–8131–0307–X

Contents

Editor's Preface

THE OLD SOUTH was a "body politic" in the elemental if not the technical sense of the expression. Politics largely served the region as a shield against outside threats to its institutions, especially against threats to its "peculiar institution"—slavery. The premier architect of this shield was John C. Calhoun of South Carolina, who expounded the doctrines of state nullification, a regional veto on national legislation, and, as a final measure of self-preservation, secession. These doctrines eventually led to actual secession, defeat in the Civil War, the sequel known as Reconstruction, and the overthrow of Reconstruction by a resurgent South dedicated to white supremacy and regional merger into the nation's industrial and commercial mainstream.

Robert F. Durden tells concisely and ably the story of southern politics from Jeffersonian liberalism to Bourbon conservatism, all stages, ironically, rooted in states' rights. As his title indicates, he emphasizes the role of southern politics in its intractable support first of slavery and then of racism. His closing sentence illustrates with shocking clarity the enduring dilemma of a democratic society: how to reconcile its ideals with the will of the people when the two are in conflict. He says, "The South's greatest enemy in the nineteenth century . . . proved all too sadly to be the great majority of southern whites."

Because southern politics has both reflected and affected all other aspects of southern life, the present study is essential to "New Perspectives on the South." The series is designed to give a fresh and comprehensive view of the region's history as seen in the light of recent developments in the South and the nation. Each volume is expected to represent both a synthesis of the best scholarship on the topic and the author's own interpretive analysis. Twenty or more volumes are planned.

Charles P. Roland

Preface

THE AMERICAN SOUTH in the nineteenth century moved politically from a predominantly nationalistic, optimistic mood in the Jeffersonian era to a sullenly sectional, chronically defensive attitude in the decades after the Civil War. As much a two-party region as any other part of the nation in the middle decades of the antebellum period, the South emerged from the experience of Reconstruction with the one-party domination of the Democrats. After furnishing a disproportionate share of top national leadership in the early days of the republic, the South in the latter portion of the century provided no nationally outstanding political leaders at all. Southern politics, as the most important and comprehensive institutional expression of the southern electorate's collective hopes and fears, sharply reflected that transition from buoyant nationalism to aggrieved sectionalism, from two-party competition to Democratic hegemony. The illumination and elaboration of that theme is the central purpose of this volume.

Its thesis is that the single greatest cause of the essentially tragic political fate of the South in the nineteenth century was a self-inflicted wound: the gradual surrender of the southern white majority, beginning in the 1820s, to the pride, fears, and hates of racism. Before the Civil War that racism expressed itself primarily in the attachment to and increasingly fervid defense of black slavery. After the war white southerners sought and ultimately found other ways to assert white dominance over the black minority.

Political historians of the South, expecially within the past decade, have emphatically articulated a central fact that was only dimly or partially understood earlier: that nineteenth-century southerners, just as much as northerners, were the proud heirs of the American Revolution and its republican ideology of liberty, property, and equal rights. In the case of the South, however, that liberty came increasingly to mean, especially from the 1820s on, the freedom to own slave property, and later the freedom to take that property to the nation's territories in the West. While that particular type of property was held by only a minority of white southerners, the nonslaveholding majority came increasingly to believe that only the enslavement of the blacks made possible the ostensible liberty and equality of all whites, slaveholders and non-slaveholders alike.

Banking, internal improvements, Indian policy, innumerable state or local issues—all these and a myriad of other matters were the staples of southern politics in the antebellum South. But as the possible ban on the expansion of slavery—or, to be more accurate, the ban on slaveholders' right to carry slave property into federal territory—rose to the center of national attention during and after the Mexican War, the South's peculiar racial modification or adaptation of the republican ideology began to grow ominously clear. Events in the winter of 1860–1861, following the presidential victory of an all-northern political party pledged to the denial of this right, made even clearer the white southerners' definition of liberty and equal rights.

I am particularly grateful to Dewey Grantham and Paul Escott, among others, for their helpful suggestions about this book. I am also indebted to the two anonymous readers of the original draft of the manuscript, from whose perceptive suggestions I hope the book has benefited.

As in many earlier cases, I also appreciate the excellent and ever-dependable assistance of Mrs. Vivian Jackson.

CHAPTER ONE

The Jeffersonian Ascendancy
1800–1828

To say that most articulate southerners were ardently nationalistic during, and for quite a while after, Thomas Jefferson's presidency is not to imply that they were not also conscious of certain sectional interests more or less peculiar to the South. Like other Americans, with New Englanders being perhaps the most conspicuous example, southerners first became conscious of their sectional interests as their nationalism was born during the American Revolution.

The necessity of intercolonial and then interstate cooperation in the long struggle for independence first schooled Americans in the rich diversity of the nation and the constant difficulty of harmonizing differences. The diversity was born not only out of geographical and climatic differences but also out of the profoundly varied histories of thirteen colonies that became proud new states as the Revolution proceeded. Just as New Englanders learned, to their dismay, that the matter of the Newfoundland fisheries was of less than burning concern to most other Americans, southerners quickly became aware that the exportation of certain agricultural products—originally tobacco, rice, and indigo—was a matter of the utmost importance primarily to them.

To take another example, and one more central and portentous for the nineteenth century, slavery existed in all of the colonies as the Revolution began. But it barely existed in most of the New England states and was already heavily concentrated in the states of Maryland, Virginia, North and South Carolina, and Georgia.

1

The first census in 1790 revealed that about 90 percent of the three-quarter million blacks in the United States lived in the South, where most were slaves and where they constituted over a third (36.4 percent) of the population. In New England, in contrast, blacks constituted 1.7 percent of the population, and in the mid-Atlantic states, 5.3 percent. While such exact data are lacking for the Revolutionary era, the picture would not be essentially different. One of the early and serious quarrels among the Americans gathered in the Continental Congress during the Revolution concerned the apportioning of taxes among the states according to population. In determining population, should the slaves be counted as persons? Or were they merely property? In this instance, northerners insisted that the slaves be counted as persons, while southerners retorted that the slaves were first and foremost property. Why, the southerners asked, should their particular kind of property lead to an increase in their tax load while the ships, warehouses, and various other types of mercantile wealth in the North went unnoticed and untaxed?

This particular quarrel, which illustrates how nationalism and sectionalism were born concurrently and even symbiotically in the United States, had important, long-lasting repercussions. As a result of southern objections to the counting of slaves as persons, the Articles of Confederation provided for the central government to requisition contributions (taxes) from the states on the basis of private lands and their improvements. When adequate revenues were still not forthcoming, the Confederation Congress in 1783 again turned to the idea of basing requisitions to the states on population, with slaves to be counted. Southerners, of course, once again objected. When someone suggested a compromise whereby two slaves might be counted as one person, Congress began playing a numbers game, with northerners pressing for a high slave count and southerners for the opposite. When James Madison of Virginia finally proposed that five slaves be counted as three persons in determining population, Congress approved the compromise, and the amendment to the Articles of Confederation was sent to the states for ratification. Unanimity was required for ratification, however, and since it was not achieved, the amendment died.

In 1787 the Constitutional Convention finally settled the most serious crisis it faced by the great compromise between the large and small states, whereby the Senate would be composed of two senators from each state, regardless of size, and the House of Representatives would be based on population. In the most important sectional compromise dealing with slavery, the framers of the Constitution provided further that "Representatives and direct taxes" were to be apportioned among the states according to the size of the free population plus "three-fifths of all other persons," the latter phrase being a euphemism for slaves.

Ironically, northerners and southerners tended to reverse themselves—or swap positions—when the matter of counting slaves as persons became a matter of political power. Through the three-fifths compromise, the South immediately gained additional seats not only in the House of Representatives but also in the electoral college, since the Constitution assigned each state the same number of presidential electors as it had senators and representatives. The new federal government barely got under way in 1789 before some northerners began to express unhappiness about the three-fifths compromise, and in the nineteenth century the objections and complaints grew ever greater.

For all of the practical differences between the northern and southern states on the matter of slavery, however, the most important fact about the institution in the last quarter of the eighteenth century and well into the Jeffersonian era was that there existed, at least among articulate Americans, a national consensus about it. The consensus was an ambiguous one, and it was implicitly, and sometimes explicitly, racist. Yet its existence made possible the writing of the Constitution, the launching of the federal government, and the formation of national, intersectional political parties.

Many Americans, southerners as well as northerners, began to grow uneasy about slavery during the American Revolution. Fighting for liberty and committed to an ideology based on the

God-given natural rights of mankind, Americans had to acknowledge an embarrassing gap between their revolutionary ideals and
the reality of slavery. In the North, one state after another, beginning during the Revolution, proceeded to abolish slavery. By the
time New Jersey and New York launched their plans for gradual
emancipation in 1799 and 1804, respectively, the Mason-Dixon
line separating Maryland from Pennsylvania had become the de-
marcation between free and slave states. Slavery, in short, became
peculiar to the South and, increasingly in the nineteenth century,
would be referred to as the South's "peculiar institution."

Many southern leaders of the Revolutionary generation were
forced for the first time to think long and carefully about slavery,
and most of them joined in denouncing the institution. As early
as 1764 a prominent Virginian, Arthur Lee, declared, "It is evi-
dent that the bondage we have imposed on the African is abso-
lutely repugnant to justice." In the next decade Patrick Henry
frankly confessed his dilemma: "Would anyone believe that I am
master of slaves of my own purchase? I am drawn along by the
general inconvenience of living here without them. I will not, I
cannot justify it."

Thomas Jefferson emerged as the most famous of the South's
critics of slavery in the Revolutionary era, yet neither he nor any
other southern leader actually moved to follow the northern lead
in gradually abolishing the institution. Many southerners expressed the *hope* that some day, somehow, slavery might be ended,
but actions against the deeply rooted institution never quite
matched words. For southerners, and for most northerners who
considered the South's dilemma, slavery there had become a "necessary evil," a regrettable but inescapable necessity for social,
economic, and racial reasons.

This national consensus concerning slavery in the South
meant that northerners, while free to abolish the relatively puny
institution in their own states, felt no compulsion to attack southerners for not doing likewise. Southerners, for their part, admitted the embarrassment and incongruity of slavery's existence
among a people dedicated to liberty and freedom. Thus the ques-

tion of slavery, when it inevitably arose during the Constitutional Convention of 1787, could be dealt with coolly and without rancor; compromises were possible, not only about counting three-fifths of the slaves as persons but also about denying the new federal government, for twenty years only, the power to move against the importation of slaves from Africa or other foreign sources. Southerners could also accept the fact that the Northwest Ordinance of 1787 prohibited the introduction of slavery into the territory north of the Ohio river. Not until the 1820s would there be a challenge to the national consensus concerning slavery in the South as a necessary evil. And that challenge to and eventual break with the older consensus came first from the South. For almost two decades before that began to happen, however, southerners experienced what was for most of them a happy integration or meshing of their sectional interests with national policies and programs.

As the first party system emerged in the 1790s in response to Alexander Hamilton's economic policies and to the foreign policy dilemmas confronting the young nation, the South spawned both Federalists and Republicans. While the former were strong in Baltimore, Richmond, Charleston, other commercial centers, and the Shenandoah Valley, the Anti-Federalist or Republican party of Thomas Jefferson and James Madison had the greater attraction for the agrarian majority in the South. This fact became even clearer after Jefferson won the presidential election of 1800 and proceeded deftly, especially during his first term, to cut the ground from beneath his political opponents.

Politics in the early nineteenth century remained the prerogative of property-owning, adult, free males, for political democracy, as people in the nineteenth century would come to define the term, had not arrived. The older, more populous states of Virginia, North Carolina, and South Carolina allowed a man to vote only if he owned a certain amount of land or was a taxpayer. By 1820 only Maryland, Kentucky, and the new state of Alabama permitted all white adult males to vote. In most southern states property qualifications for officeholding further restricted democracy, and the old practice of oral, public voting, which Virginia and Kentucky long retained, no doubt had an inhibiting effect on the electoral process.

The political institution with which southerners had the most direct and frequent contact was the governing body of the county, known generally as the county court. In most states it was a self-perpetuating, nonelective body composed of the leading landholders in the county. By the 1820s only in Georgia and the newer states of Louisiana and Alabama could the voters elect the powerful members of the county governing bodies.

Just as political power lay upward on the socioeconomic scale in the hands of landowning farmers and planters, so too, in a geographical sense, did the older, eastern portions of the seaboard states hold a disproportionate share of power. The state legislatures not only named most state officials, including the governor in some states, but also elected the United States senators and presidential electors. Service in the legislature was often a virtual prerequisite for election as a representative or senator in the United States Congress. By giving each county equal representation in the legislature, regardless of the size of the county's white population, or by using the federal three-fifths formula for determining population, or by various other methods, the eastern or low-country portions of the seaboard states, where the largest number of planters and slaves were concentrated, long managed to wield a disproportionate power in political affairs. Although Jefferson did not fear political democracy as so many of his contemporaries did, it had by no means been achieved during his presidency, and internal political battles about democratization— at least for white adult males—would begin to produce marked changes in most of the South by the 1820s and 1830s.

Among those southerners who could vote in the early years of the century, the Jeffersonian Republicans increased their popularity with a series of measures. The repeal in March 1802 of the unpopular Hamiltonian excise taxes, for example, was favored by all members of the House of Representatives from Maryland, Georgia, Tennessee, and Kentucky, and a great majority of those from Virginia, North Carolina, and South Carolina. In the South the single most popular Jeffersonian action, however, was the purchase of the Louisiana Territory from France in 1803. Overcoming scruples about the strict interpretation of the Constitution, which made no explicit provision for doubling the size of the nation through the acquisition of real-estate, even at a fire-sale price, Jefferson envisioned a transcontinental republic filled with land-owning farmers.

Precisely such a vision infuriated his Federalist foes, increasingly centered in New England and caught up in a frenzied sectional mania against Jefferson and all that he stood for. One particularly embittered group of Federalists, known as the Essex Junto, schemed with Vice President Aaron Burr to have him elected governor of New York so that he might lead that state to secede alongside the New England states. The plot aborted, but Federalist resentment against alleged southern domination of the federal government continued unabated. To reduce the South's political power, the legislature of Massachusetts proposed an amendment to the Constitution providing that representation in the United States House of Representatives be based only on the number of free inhabitants of the states. Among other southern protests, Georgia called the proposed abandonment of one of the important compromises of 1787 not only unjust but one calculated to disorganize the Union. Other states also responded unfavorably, but in some northern quarters, especially among Federalists, hostility to the three-fifths compromise remained very much alive.

That the agrarian nationalism and expansionism of the Jeffersonian Republicans appealed to voters in all parts of the country, not just in the South and West, is indicated by the results of the presidential election of 1804. The Federalist candidate, Charles Cotesworth Pinckney of South Carolina, won the electoral votes of only Connecticut and Delaware plus two of Maryland's. Thomas Jefferson, in other words, carried all sections, with 162 electoral votes to 14 for his opponent.

During Jefferson's second term, foreign affairs brought mounting woes to the United States. With Great Britain and France engaged in the mortal combat of the Napoleonic War, the

United States as a neutral and maritime nation eager to engage in world trade found itself buffeted by both European powers. Through the controversial Embargo Act, the Jefferson administration attempted to use the economic pressure of a boycott on exports to force concessions from the British or French or from both. The measure not only failed to do that but produced widespread economic distress in various parts of the United States, most conspicuously in the port cities of New England, where talk of secession intensified and the Federalists gained strength. Even in the South, where Republicans were in firm control, opposition to the embargo mounted, and one of Jefferson's last measures before yielding the presidency to his long-time friend and secretary of state, James Madison, in March 1809 was to sign the act repealing the measure.

The war with Britain which Jefferson had so desperately avoided finally came in 1812, when President Madison yielded to the clamor of the Congressional "War Hawks," the young Republicans from the West and South who staunchly defended the nation's neutral rights while also covetously eyeing Britain's Canada and Spain's Florida. Frontier anger about British dealing with the Indians also played a part in bringing about the war, as one of the War Hawks, Felix Grundy of Tennessee, explained: "We shall drive the British from our Continent—they will no longer have an opportunity of intriguing with our Indian neighbors, and setting on the ruthless savage to tomahawk our women and children." Henry Clay of Kentucky, John C. Calhoun of South Carolina, William Crawford of Georgia, and others were in the strident vanguard of the Republican congressmen who wanted and got a "Second War of Independence" against the former mother country.

The vote on the war resolution in the House of Representatives was seventy-nine for and forty-nine against. While congressmen from the frontier areas of New England joined those from Pennsylvania, the South, and the West in supporting the war, the opposition came largely from the maritime, commercial, and Federalist areas of New England, New York, and New Jersey. The even closer vote in the Senate, nineteen to thirteen, also reflected the fact that a divided nation had embarked on a war that increased both southern nationalism and angry sectionalism among Federalists in New England.

Except for John Randolph and John Taylor of Virginia, Nathaniel Macon of North Carolina, and a small handful of other doctrinaire Republicans, most of the southern Republicans in the two decades after 1800 greatly deemphasized the constitutional principles of states' rights, strict interpretation, and strictly limited power for the federal government. Those were the major themes advanced by Thomas Jefferson and James Madison in the resolutions endorsed in 1798 by the legislatures of Virginia and Kentucky as part of the protest against the Alien and Sedition laws enacted by the Federalists and as part of the Republican campaign that brought Jefferson to the presidency in 1800. If most Republicans subsequently ignored those principles of 1798, the Federalists certainly did not, for in mounting crescendo from the time of the Louisiana Purchase through the Embargo Act and climaxing in the War of 1812, the Federalists employed the weapons forged by Jefferson and Madison in 1798 to oppose those two presidents and the major policies of their administrations.

Secession threats from New England Federalists began early in Jefferson's first term, with the Louisiana Purchase especially inspiring a flurry of them. When Louisiana, the first state to be carved from the Purchase, was ready for statehood in 1811, one of the leading Federalist spokesmen, Josiah Quincy of Massachusetts, used language that would be echoed later in debates about Texas: "It is my deliberate opinion that, if this bill [to admit Louisiana] passes, the bonds of this Union are virtually dissolved; that the states which compose it are free from their original obligations, and that, as it will be the right of all, so it will be the duty of some, definitely to prepare for a separation—amicably if they can, violently if they must."

The unpopularity of the second war with Britain among New England's Federalists nurtured even stronger threats of disunionism. But when the Federalists of New England responded to Massachusetts' call for a convention at Hartford, Connecticut, late in 1814, moderates prevented any move toward secession.

The convention instead demanded constitutional amendments which would, among other things, restrict a president to one term, require a two-thirds majority in Congress to admit new states or declare war, and abolish the three-fifths compromise.

Both the patriotic and the partisan sensibilities of southern Republicans were outraged by the antiwar activities and disunionist rhetoric of the New England Federalists. Before the convention at Hartford actually met and proved to be less extreme than expected, one of the leading Republican newspapers, the *Richmond* (Virginia) *Enquirer*, declared: "*The Union* is in danger. . . . No man, no association of men, no state or set of states has a right to withdraw itself from the Union of its own accord. The same power which knit us together, can only un-knit. . . . *The majority of states* which formed the Union must consent to the withdrawal of *any one branch of it*. Until *that* consent has been obtained, any attempt to dissolve the Union, or obstruct the efficiency of its constitutional laws, is Treason."

The undoing of the Federalists came not from such southern Republican censure and constitutional reasoning, however, but from events themselves. Reports of the Hartford Convention appeared in the nation's newspapers alongside stories about two even more startling developments: General Andrew Jackson's dramatic defeat of the British in the battle of New Orleans early in 1815 and the signing of the peace treaty between the United States and Great Britain at Ghent, Belgium, late in 1814. Quickly forgetting about the various reverses and humiliations the United States had suffered during the controversial war, most Americans fervently celebrated their "winning" of a war that in reality had not settled much. The optimistic nationalism and governmental activism of the Republicans, now more dominant than ever, soared to new heights as the fortunes of the Federalists sank even further.

Despite lingering constitutional scruples that led Presidents James Madison and James Monroe to call in vain for amendments that would clearly legitimize certain activities by the federal government, such as the chartering of a central bank or the building of turnpikes, the Republican leaders in Congress were willing to have the federal government act on several fronts without waiting for the slow and problematical outcome of the amending process. Since the expiration in 1811 of the charter of the Bank of the United States, whose original launching then-Secretary of State Thomas Jefferson had strongly opposed in 1791, the Republicans encountered embarrassing difficulties in financing the War of 1812; a plethora of unsound banknotes in circulation also helped dramatize the need for the control and order that a central bank could provide. President Madison addressed the need in his annual message to Congress in 1815, and John C. Calhoun introduced the bill to charter a second Bank of the United States in 1816. The bill passed the House by a vote of eighty to seventy-one, with over half of the favorable votes coming from the southern states. The tobacco-producing planters of Virginia and Maryland and a few other southern groups opposed the rechartering of the bank, but the most vocal southern hostility to the institution would not come until after the panic of 1819 and Chief Justice John Marshall's sweepingly nationalist and Hamiltonian decision in *McCulloch* vs. *Maryland*, which among other things upheld the federal government's power to charter the bank and denied the right of Maryland (and by implication any other state) to tax it or any of its branches.

While there clearly were differences among southerners about the bank, southern opinion and leaders were even more divided on the question of a protective tariff. Ironically in light of Jefferson's own agrarian bias, his embargo policy and more especially the war that followed under Madison stimulated manufacturing in the United States. Especially in New England, the number of spindles for producing cotton yarn jumped dramatically, and the first mill in the nation to add to the spindles a power loom for weaving was built in Massachusetts in 1814. While Calhoun and other southern Republicans supported the tariff act of 1816, which placed a 25 percent duty on cotton goods and certain other manufactured items imported from abroad, the majority of the southern members of the House of Representatives (thirty-four out of fifty-seven) voted against the measure. The depth of the rancor and divisiveness that would gradually be inspired by the tariff question was certainly not, however, apparent in 1816 as

the federal government embarked on the explicit program of encouraging the growth of American manufacturing.

Alongside the new tariff and the central bank, many Republicans envisioned a bold program for encouraging internal improvements—turnpikes, canals, and other facilities for better
communication and transportation. The *Richmond Enquirer* in
September 1815 typified the spirit and thinking of many in the
exuberant era: "Have the Americans no water courses to clear, no
canals to construct, no roads to form, no bridges to erect? Must
the productions of our soil be continually subject to obstructions
on the way to market? Must our want of internal communication
forever remain the laughing-stock of strangers and the reproach
of our citizens? . . . Let us seize this precious moment and devote
it to *Internal Improvements*. Now is the time for Virginia to extend
her character and preserve her influence in the union. Let us
adopt some scheme of gradual improvement and go on without
ceasing."

As with the bank, Calhoun, strongly supported by Henry
Clay and other former War Hawks, took the lead in introducing
a bill to establish a permanent fund for internal improvements
from the income the federal government expected to derive from
its one-fifth interest in the capital stock of the Bank of the United
States and from the $1.5 million bonus the bank was required to
pay for its charter. The bill passed by the narrowest of margins
but was vetoed by President Madison, who in this case held out
for an amendment to the Constitution explicitly granting the federal government the power to assist in the construction of turnpikes and canals. While federal involvement in this area was
temporarily blocked by Madison's veto, the idea remained much
alive and was destined to become a vital part of the "American
System" which would increasingly be identified with Henry Clay
and his followers in future years.

Beneath the nationalist rhetoric and policies of the era's most
prominent southern leaders, such as Calhoun and Clay, there existed serious differences among southerners concerning not only
such matters as the Bank of the United States, the tariff, and
internal improvements but also local and state matters, such as

qualifications for voting and officeholding, legislative apportionment, and taxation. Just as there were marked differences between the national policies favored by majorities in the older seaboard states and those preferred in the newer states of what was then the Southwest, so within the states themselves there were sharp divisions between those of the tidewater or low country and those of the piedmont or up-country, or, as in Tennessee, between the mountainous eastern and the cotton-producing western parts of the state. In short, beneath the facade of Republican consensus in the so-called Era of Good Feeling there existed not one unified and self-conscious South but many varied and often conflicting groups of southerners. Political unity for the South in the federal arena developed, however temporarily, only when slavery, the South's peculiar institution, came under sudden and sharp attack in 1819.

Missouri Territory's petition for statehood seemed, in its early stages at least, to be quite routine. Settled initially by pioneers mostly from nearby slaveholding states, the proposed new state would have a population of about 60,000, including some 10,000 slaves, and the majority of Missourians assumed that slavery would be continued under statehood. But when the bill dealing with Missouri came before the House of Representatives early in 1819, Representative James Tallmadge, Jr., of New York introduced an amendment that would prohibit the further importation of slaves into Missouri and provide for the gradual emancipation of any children born to slaves already there. The Tallmadge amendment, in short, would grant statehood to Missouri only if it gradually became a free state.

Sectional political battles, especially relating to slavery, had gone on since the American Revolution but never on such a dramatic and prolonged scale as those inspired by the Tallmadge amendment. Although Louisiana had been admitted in 1812 as a slave state carved from the vast Louisiana Purchase, a small portion of it lay east of the Mississippi, whereas Missouri would be the first state wholly west of that vast river and symbolic dividing line. Supporters of the Tallmadge amendment emphasized that point and insisted that they merely wished to reaffirm for the trans-Mississippi West the principle of antislavery extension embodied in the Northwest Ordinance of 1787. Their most striking argument, however, was a strong, even impassioned, attack on the institution of slavery as morally wrong on humanitarian and biblical grounds and inconsistent with the deepest philosophical principles embodied in the Declaration of Independence and the basic democratic foundations of the nation. Echoing Representative Tallmadge and his supporters, northern newspapers spoke out against slavery as never before, one declaring that the "*slavery of man* is abhorrent to every noble and honorable feeling." Another asserted that "slavery is contrary to the spirit of our republican institutions—in its effects subversive of the prosperity and best interests of society . . . [and] it is the duty of every good citizen to use all constitutional and proper means to procure its melioration, and to prevent its extension."

In light of the sudden and widespread attack on what had become by 1819 a peculiarly southern institution, the most significant aspect of the response by southerners in and out of Congress was a refusal to defend the institution itself. Still committed to the old idea of slavery as a necessary evil, most articulate southerners joined their opponents in deploring human bondage. In Congress a Georgian avowed his unhappiness about slavery and insisted that he would hail the day that saw "the black population of the United States placed upon the high eminence of equal rights." The governor of Virginia declared: "the deplorable error of our ancestors in copying a civil institution from savage Africa, has fixed upon their posterity a depressing burden." The editor of the *Richmond Enquirer* spoke similarly: "We protest . . . that we do not vindicate servitude; we wish no slave had touched our soil; we wish it could be terminated. As republicans, we frankly declare before our God and our country, that we abhor its institution." Southerners frequently coupled such protestations with the ingenious argument that allowing slavery to expand would help dilute the evil and possibly accelerate abolition.

Refusing, then, to defend slavery, the southern spokesmen chose to fight on the constitutional grounds that Congress possessed no power to place binding restrictions upon a state as it entered the Union. While the northerners pointed to the antislavery aspect of the Northwest Ordinance, southerners recalled the fundamental promise of that trail-blazing legislation: territories were to evolve into new states that were to be admitted into the Union on a basis of full equality with the original thirteen states. In answer to northern state legislatures that endorsed the Tallmadge amendment, the Kentucky lower house insisted that if Congress could "trammel or control the powers of a territory in the formation of a state government, that body may, on the same principles, reduce its powers to little more than those possessed by the people of the District of Columbia; and whilst professing to make it a sovereign state, may bind it in a perpetual vassalage, and reduce it to the condition of a province."

The South, so staunchly nationalistic since 1800, found itself in the Missouri debates of 1819–1820 championing states' rights and strict interpretation of the Constitution. At the same time, the New Englanders, who for two decades had sought to limit and obstruct federal power, now joined other northerners in supporting a liberal interpretation of the Constitution and the extension of federal power. Yet the fact that Missouri was applying for statehood was crucial for the South's case and helped it win over some support from northerners.

The Tallmadge amendment's ban on the introduction into Missouri of additional slaves initially passed the House of Representatives in 1819 by a starkly sectional vote of eighty-seven to seventy-six, all but one member from the slave states voting against it and all but ten from the free states supporting it. In the House, the fact that population growth in the North had outstripped that in the South was reflected in the fact that there were already 105 members from the free states and only 81 from the slave states. In the Senate, as all those interested in national politics became acutely aware during the Missouri debates, the balance between free and slave states had so far been maintained, with eleven of each. In that body the Tallmadge amendment was defeated, and when neither House nor Senate would modify its position, Congress adjourned without acting on the Missouri question.

Newspapers, legislatures, and various other bodies in both sections of the country joined in the debate. Stung by the vehemence and suddenness of the northern attack on slavery, some southerners suspected a deep-laid conspiracy, perhaps on the part of the die-hard Federalists. There was no conspiracy, but inevitably intertwined with the moral and humanitarian attack on an institution for which even southerners still apologized there certainly was a great deal of plain old sectional politics. For one thing, some northerners were frank in their explanation that they did not wish to see slavery extended because that would mean the simultaneous extension of the three-fifths compromise, which New England Federalists especially had railed against with increasing rancor since 1800. Senator Rufus King of Massachusetts, one of the strong supporters of the Tallmadge amendment, pointed out that the abrogation of the three-fifths clause would mean the loss to the South of twenty representatives and therefore twenty presidential electors. Virginia, especially resented in some quarters as the home of three successive two-term presidents, would alone forfeit seven representatives if three-fifths of her slaves were not included in her population count. King charged that the clause had given to the slave states a preponderance over the other states, but "the extension of this disproportionate power to the new states would be unjust and odious."

In addition to the northern hostility to the three-fifths clause, another political aspect of the Missouri struggle lay in the fact that the nearly two decades of Republican ascendancy had been based in large part on an agrarian alliance of the South and West, with the new states north of the Ohio River included in the latter. The Tallmadge amendment, however, sharply broke that pattern and saw the rapidly growing states of the Old Northwest aligned with the East. Confiding to his diary, Secretary of State John Quincy Adams prophetically noted that the Missouri debate "disclosed a secret: it revealed the basis for a new organization of parties. . . . Here was a new party ready formed, . . . terrible to the whole Union, but portentously terrible to the South— threatening in its progress the emancipation of all their slaves, threatening in its immediate effect that Southern domination which has swayed the Union for the last twenty years, and threatening that political ascendancy of Virginia, upon which Clay and Crawford both had fastened their principal hopes of personal aggrandizement."

For all of Adams's prescience, his scenario was premature by several decades. When Congress convened again late in 1819 and the earlier deadlock about the Tallmadge amendment continued between the House and the Senate, political leaders intent on saving the Republican party and ending the dangerous sectional impasse went to work. Since Maine had earlier sought to be separated from Massachusetts and admitted as a new state, the compromisers proposed that Congress admit both Missouri and Maine without restriction, that is, with federal silence concerning whatever constitutional arrangements either new state wished to make concerning slavery. But since it was widely understood that Maine would enter as a free state and Missouri as a slave state, the balance between the two categories would be maintained in the Senate. Further, the compromisers proposed and the congressional majority agreed that north of the line of 36 degrees, 30 minutes in the remainder of the Louisiana Territory, slavery was to be prohibited.

The expectation at that time was that only one additional state (Arkansas) could be formed from the region south of the line, the present state of Oklahoma then being envisioned as the Indian Territory. North of the line, however, a large number of free states could be expected eventually. Consequently, many southern congressmen refused to support the compromise measure, which nevertheless passed, ending the principal phase of the drawn-out crisis.

While political leaders and some newspaper editors in both sections became deeply excited by the Missouri crisis, ordinary folk did not seem to be much aroused by the matter. Thomas Jefferson, however, followed the debate from his mountain-top home near Charlottesville, and to a political ally in Massachusetts he declared: "But this momentous question, like a fire-bell in the night, awakened and filled me with terror. I considered it at once as the knell of the Union. It is hushed, indeed, for the moment.

17

But this is a reprieve only, not a final sentence. A geographical line, coinciding with a marked principle, moral and political, once conceived and held up to the angry passions of men, will never be obliterated; and every new irritation will mark it deeper and deeper."

Jefferson went on to insist that there was "not a man on earth who would sacrifice more than I would to relieve us from this heavy reproach [of slaveholding], in any *practicable* way. The cession of that kind of property, for so it is misnamed, is a bagatelle which would not cost me a second thought, if, in that way, a general emancipation and *expatriation* could be effected; and, gradually, and with due sacrifices, I think it might be. But as it is, we have the wolf by the ears, and we can neither hold him, nor safely let him go. Justice is in one scale, and self-preservation in the other."

In the aftermath of the Missouri Compromise, how many other southerners, if any, joined Jefferson in brooding about the South's having "the wolf by the ears" no one knows. What is clear is that the episode was fraught with significance for the history of southern politics. The old opposition of New England Federalists to the three-fifths clause had now spread to a larger, even if amorphous, northern constituency and was thoroughly intertwined with opposition to the extension of slavery on the grounds that the institution was morally wrong. Furthermore, the agrarian alliance between the South and the original Northwest had been shattered, at least temporarily, by the Tallmadge amendment.

Perhaps most important of all, the Missouri crisis dramatized for many southerners what only a few far-sighted ones had realized earlier: that the South, instead of having roughly half of the nation's population, as in the beginning of the national era, had become a minority section. Already significantly outnumbered in the House of Representatives, southerneres became more conscious than ever of the importance of trying to maintain a balance in the Senate.

Just as the Missouri affair only temporarily disrupted the nationally based Republican party, so it only briefly submerged southern nationalism in a strongly sectional, states-rightist defense of Missouri's right to have slavery if Missourians so wished—or, to put the matter differently, the denial of the federal government's constitutional right to prevent a state from instituting slavery as the state entered the Union. The storm, like one on a sultry summer day, had blown up suddenly and raged fiercely, at least on the congressional level. But it had passed relatively quickly, too, and the great majority of southerners, like their northern counterparts, seemed quite willing to live with the compromise and get back to business—and politics—as usual.

But neither business nor politics could operate "as usual" in the early 1820s because of the Panic of 1819 and the ensuing economic depression that began in the same year as the Missouri debate. The European market for American exports, particularly for cotton and tobacco in the case of the South, boomed as the Napoleonic Wars ended in 1815. American agriculturalists responded to the high prices for their crops by expanding production, often by borrowing money. State banks, especially in the South and West, were all too eager to oblige their customers, and the new second Bank of the United States, eager to win friends and silence enemies, followed in its first year or so of operation a highly generous—and dangerously loose—policy of encouraging and helping the state banks.

By 1819, however, Europe's demand for American staples had drastically diminished, and commodity prices fell accordingly. Whereas cotton, which was quickly becoming the great staple of the Deep South, had been selling for thirty-three cents a pound, by the autumn of 1819 the price was about halved. Tobacco prices fell even more precipitously, and prices of pork, flour, and other commodities tumbled. Caught in debts that did not shrink alongside prices, farmers and planters alike were mired in grindingly hard times.

To make matters worse, at least from the standpoint of the debtors, the Bank of the United States repented of its initial laxity and launched a series of retrenchment measures beginning in mid-1818. As the central bank pressed the state banks for repayment in specie, the latter faced the necessity of collecting overdue debts. Many state banks, unable to meet their obligations to the Bank of the United States, suspended specie payments.

Though the causes of the depression were many and complex, the inevitable human reaction to such a series of economic woes as those produced by the Panic of 1819 was to seek an identifiable scapegoat. In the eyes of countless southerners and westerners, the ideal candidate for that distinction was the Philadelphia-based Bank of the United States and its branches scattered across the country. Using language that would echo among the Populists at the end of the century, Senator Thomas Hart Benton of Missouri levied a classic charge against the bank: "All the flourishing cities of the West are mortgaged to this money power. They may be devoured by it at any moment. They are in the jaws of the monster! A lump of butter in the mouth of a dog! One gulp, one swallow, and all is gone!" From such enmity to the Bank of the United States to hostility to the eastern cities, where lived most of those who owned the four-fifths of its stock that was privately owned, was not a big leap.

In addition to arousing western and southern hostility to the eastern "money power," the bank's alleged role in causing the depression affected southern politics in another way. Except for a small group of rigid and doctrinaire Old Republicans, such as John Randolph and John Taylor, most southerners in the heady years of the War of 1812 and its immediate aftermath had simply not been interested in the logic-chopping and legalistic hair-splitting that often characterized the constitutional interpretations of the states-rightists and strict-constructionists. Their natural stomping ground had seemed to be Federalist New England. Just as the bank question was becoming more politically volatile in and after 1819, however, Chief Justice John Marshall, in *Mc-Culloch* vs. *Maryland*, led the Supreme Court in a sweepingly nationalistic defense of the bank and the federal government's implied power to charter it—along with a categorical denial of the states' right to tax the bank or any of its branches. Not only did the decision make those who disliked the bank turn their anger toward Marshall also, but the whole question of whether the Constitution should be interpreted strictly or loosely, and the related matter of states' rights, acquired a new immediacy and urgency for a growing number of southerners.

Just as the depression helped make the bank and its policies a political and constitutional issue, so also did the Panic of 1819 affect another part of the Young Republicans' American System, the protective tariff policy that had been launched in 1816. The nation's relatively small but burgeoning corps of manufacturers responded to the hard times by clamoring for even higher protective duties. Congressmen from the Middle Atlantic states and from Ohio and Kentucky favored higher duties; New England's sentiments and votes were divided between the older shipping interests, who opposed higher duties, and the rising manufacturing element; and the staple-exporting South Atlantic states were strongly opposed to higher duties. Despite the strenuous efforts of Henry Clay, who was Speaker of the House and who championed the Kentucky hemp-growers' interest in protection for their cash crop, the opponents of the proposed steep increase in protective duties narrowly held the line in 1820.

Congressional reapportionment in 1823, however, gave the states of the Middle Atlantic and Ohio Valley regions a total of nineteen new seats. While nine new seats also went to the southwestern states, where opinions about the tariff were yet fluid and divided, the South Atlantic states gained no new seats. With the increased support for protection, Clay and his allies tried again—and more successfully—in 1824. Despite the almost solid opposition to the increased duties from the South (with the exception of Maryland, Kentucky, and Tennessee), the measure passed Congress.

For the first time in an extended, serious way, the question of the constitutionality of protectionism was raised by a Virginia congressman in the debates about the tariff of 1824. Since the power to encourage manufacturing was not among those explicitly granted to Congress in the Constitution, the Virginian argued that the measure violated the spirit if not the letter of the Constitution. While Clay insisted that the tariff measure rested on the plenary and undeniable power of Congress to regulate commerce with foreign nations, his opponents retorted that "regulation" hardly meant "prohibition," at least in peacetime, and that some of the duties were clearly becoming sufficiently high as virtually to prohibit certain imports from abroad. Like their Revolutionary ancestors who became deeply aroused by the British Parliament's trade and tax policies for the British empire, some southerners, especially South Carolinians, were becoming increasingly alarmed by and hostile to the protective tariff.

There were, in addition to the Bank of the United States and the tariff, other important public questions that much concerned southerners and about which they often disagreed. Concerning federal aid for internal improvements, for example, the newer states of the Southwest were closer in their views to the Northwest than to the South Atlantic states. The same was true concerning federal public-land policy, for all of the western states pushed hard for lower prices and other concessions that would assist the actual settlers or pioneers in acquiring public land. The South, in short, was by no means politically united on all of the issues of the 1820s.

Yet the fact remains that the ambitious nationalistic program of the Republicans after 1815 was not really unifying the nation, as had been the intention of Calhoun and Clay and their allies. On the contrary, the bank, the tariff, and other aspects of federal activism were promoting disunity as different sections of the country reacted to the various policies according to their local interests.

The disunity of not only the country but also the Republican party was dramatically illustrated in 1824. The presidential election of that year degenerated into a wild scramble among favorite-son candidates from all parts of the nation. While a remnant of the Republican party's congressional caucus in Washington tried to hand the nomination, and thus the presidency in a one-party situation, to William H. Crawford of Georgia, various other leading Republicans and their supporters rebelled against the system that had kept the Virginia Dynasty in power for almost a quarter of a century. Calhoun of South Carolina, Clay of Kentucky, and John Quincy Adams of Massachusetts were among the well qualified and richly experienced aspirants to the highest office in the land. General Andrew Jackson, less experienced politically than militarily, was something of a newcomer to national politics, but his name proved to be magic with rank-and-file voters in many parts of the nation.

The strange scramble brought the voters out as never before, especially in the southern states. But Jackson, the favorite of the majority of the voters, did not receive a majority of the electoral votes, and, in accordance with the Constitution, the election was thrown into the House of Representatives, where the choice had to be made from among the top three candidates. Calhoun, after discerning the strong popular trend in favor of Jackson, had withdrawn from the presidential race to run for the vice presidency. Clay, who was fourth in the electoral vote and therefore eliminated from the contest, threw his support to his fellow nationalist, John Quincy Adams, who thus became the sixth president, to the absolute dismay and disgust of Andrew Jackson's ardent champions.

Adams's ambitious and nationalistic program called for extensive internal improvements, the creation of a national university, and other federal activities and initiatives. Echoing the optimistic nationalism of the young Republicans of a decade earlier, Adams, conscientious and able but sadly lacking in political skills, presided over an administration that had no unified party support, while various groups in the South became more and more alienated from and suspicious of the federal government.

Federal appropriations for internal improvements were much larger than they had ever been but, except for the Dismal Swamp Canal between the North Carolina sounds and Chesapeake Bay, only a trivial amount of federal money for such improvements went to Virginia and not a cent to South Carolina. The legislature of the latter state protested late in 1825 that "it is an unconstitutional exercise of power, on the part of Congress, to tax the citizens of one State to make roads and canals for the citizens of another State."

But the anger of South Carolinians about federal aid for internal improvements was nothing compared to their growing fury over the protective tariff. Continuing economic stagnation, especially for the cotton producers, led South Carolinians to search for an explanation for their troubles, and more and more of them concluded that the protectionist policy was the culprit. Producing staples which were mostly sold abroad, the South Carolinians gravitated naturally toward the laissez-faire and free-trade doctrines of Adam Smith and other liberal economists. Even Vice President Calhoun, who had been a leading advocate of the protective tariff of 1816, was being forced by the tide of opinion in his home state to reverse his views.

Evidence abounded of South Carolina's mounting hostility to the tariff. The widely respected president of South Carolina College, Thomas Cooper, published a pamphlet in 1823 in which he denied the constitutionality of protectionism and advanced various other arguments against it. Other prominent South Carolinians echoed Cooper, and in 1825, in reaction to President Adams's eager nationalism, the South Carolina legislature fired off resolutions against the tariff as well as the Bank of the United States and internal improvements.

The tariff was revised upward again in 1828, a presidential election year. In fact, some all-too-clever presidential politicking in Congress helped produce a strange measure with very high duties. In South Carolina especially, but elsewhere in the South, too, the measure quickly became known as the Tariff of Abominations. The legislatures of Virginia, Georgia, and Alabama remonstrated, but the most portentous reaction came in South Carolina. Sounding like the New England Federalists of an earlier era, various South Carolina political leaders and editors began to threaten secession. One Charleston newspaper declared, for example, "The question of Disunion is at last seriously and openly submitted to the consideration of the people of South Carolina."

To head off and control such talk became an urgent necessity for Vice President Calhoun, who in 1828 again sought the same office on the ticket with Andrew Jackson for president. Secretly Calhoun wrote the "South Carolina Exposition and Protest," which the state legislature published early in 1829. It was the most formal and formidable attack on the protective policy produced up to that time, but Calhoun went far beyond merely arguing against the constitutionality of protectionism and protesting that the burden of the tariff rested on the agrarian South while the benefits went to northern manufacturers. Building on the constitutional arguments advanced by Jefferson and Madison in the Virginia and Kentucky Resolutions of 1798, Calhoun maintained that the Constitution was a compact among sovereign states and that the federal government was, in the last analysis, the creation of the states. If the federal government acted contrary to the Constitution or exceeded the powers explicitly given to it, a sovereign state, acting through a specially elected convention of its people, had not merely the right but the solemn duty of declaring the unconstitutional law null and void within the state.

Calhoun would continue later to polish and refine his nullification doctrine, but he advanced it originally as an allegedly moderate, peaceful alternative to more radical proposals that some angry South Carolinians were making in response to the tariff. As the documents of Jefferson and Madison in 1798 had been part of their campaign for the election of 1800, so too Calhoun's "Exposition and Protest" was written partly as a political document. Andrew Jackson's views on the tariff, as on most other important questions of the day, remained largely unknown in 1828. In Pennsylvania and other pro-tariff states, Jackson's supporters assured the voters that the Tennessean would support a policy that fostered American manufactures. But in the "Exposition," Calhoun praised Jackson as that "eminent citizen, distinguished for his services to his country, and his justice and patriotism." The document went on to express the hope that Jackson's administration would bring "a complete restoration of the pure principles of our Government."

As the era of Andrew Jackson began and events gradually clarified the new president's strong views on various important public questions, many, in fact most, American voters would come to believe that he had indeed restored "the pure principles" of the federal government. Ironically, Calhoun and most South Carolinians would violently disagree.

CHAPTER TWO

❧

The South and the
Second Party System
1828–1846

ALTHOUGH ANDREW JACKSON had been denied the presidency in 1824, the campaign of that year demonstrated his great popularity with the rank-and-file voters in various parts of the country, especially in the South. In the seven southern states where presidential electors were popularly chosen, the vote for Jackson in 1824 equalled the combined vote for his three opponents; and he received over half (55 out of 108) of the South's electoral votes. Georgia and Louisiana soon joined the ranks of those states where the voters rather than the legislature chose presidential electors, and only South Carolina clung to the old system.

Despite the military hero's popularity with the voters, when the election in 1824 was thrown into the House of Representatives only one-third of the southern congressmen stood by him. Although Henry Clay played a key role in helping Adams in Kentucky and other western states, in the Southeast, particularly in North Carolina, the entrenched leaders in the eastern portions of the states were suspicious of Jackson and, by supporting Crawford, indirectly helped elect Adams. That result not only left a large number of voters more determined than ever to see Jackson elected president; it also served as a stimulus for greater political democracy within the southern states, especially in the older ones of the seaboard, where voters in the up-country and mountainous regions pushed more vigorously than ever for reapportionment and an end to eastern dominance within the state legislatures.

Andrew Jackson by no means created the democratic movement that affected the South as well as other parts of the country in the 1820s. But Jackson in 1828 was clearly the beneficiary as well as the symbol of the movement. More than twice as many southern voters as in the previous election went to the polls in 1828, and Jackson and the Democratic Republicans were the strong favorites. With only New England heavily supporting Adams and the National Republicans, the Jacksonian forces had substantially recreated the prevailing coalition of the Jeffersonian era: the South and the West plus Pennsylvania and part of New York.

While Vice President Calhoun saw himself as the logical and most likely successor to the aging Jackson, the alliance between the powerful South Carolinian and the popular president grew increasingly strained. There were several reasons for this, but the most basic cause of the rift lay in the fact that Calhoun, responding to an irresistible tide of revulsion against the high protective tariff in his native South Carolina, became increasingly identified as the champion of states' rights and the foe of federal activism. Jackson, while warily quiet about the tariff, proved to be much less sympathetic to states' rights than Calhoun and others in the South had hoped.

In 1830 the two powerful leaders dramatized and publicized their break at a political banquet celebrating Jefferson's birthday. Glaring down a long table at the vice president, Jackson raised his glass and proposed a toast: "Our Federal Union: it must be preserved!" Accepting the implicit challenge, Calhoun in turn responded: "Our Federal Union—next to our liberties most dear! May we all remember that it can only be preserved by respecting the rights of the States and distributing equally the benefit and burthen of the Union!"

The rupture between Jackson and Calhoun soon became final. The president had earlier learned that back in 1818 Calhoun, then secretary of war, had argued that Jackson should be censured for his role in the campaign against the Seminole Indians in Spanish-owned Florida. The incensed Jackson reopened the matter and, dissatisfied with Calhoun's attempted explanation of the earlier episode, ended all friendly relations with the South Carolinian and increasingly committed himself to the idea of making Martin Van Buren of New York his eventual successor.

The alienation of Calhoun and his friends was a serious matter for the Democratic Republicans but posed no real threat to Jackson's reelection in 1832. With Henry Clay as the National Republicans' nominee for the presidency, the campaign became vastly enlivened by an unexpected issue. Nicholas Biddle, president of the Bank of the United States, decided early in 1832 to press immediately for the renewal of the bank's charter, although its existing charter had four years to go before it expired. Clay and Daniel Webster, both staunch friends of the bank, agreed happily with Biddle, for they calculated—quite wrongly as it turned out—that whatever Jackson, a known bank-hater, did when confronted with a bill rechartering the bank, he would be hurt politically: if he should be so "wild" as to veto the bill, his foes assumed, he would lose Pennsylvania and other northern support; on the other hand, if he signed the bill, he would lose the South.

The rechartering bill passed both the Senate and the House, with most of the negative votes coming from the South, but Jackson stunned his political foes by issuing a ringing veto message unlike any that had been known up to that point in United States history. While Jackson's constitutional objections to the bill were rather picayune, the heart of his indictment of the bank was that it enjoyed exclusive and monopolistic privileges granted by the federal government itself. In a passage that probably won him votes in 1832 and quickly became famous, Jackson affirmed his adherence to Jeffersonian principles: "There are no necessary evils in government. Its evils exist only in its abuses. If it would confine itself to equal protection, and, as Heaven does its rains, shower its favors alike on the high and the low, the rich and the poor, it would be an unqualified blessing." Jackson charged further that Congress, in attempting to gratify the desires of many of the nation's rich men to be made richer by federal actions, had "arrayed section against section, interest against interest, and man against man, in a fearful commotion which threatens to shake the foundations of our Union."

Most well-to-do Americans, especially in the commercial centers of the nation, were infuriated by Jackson's veto message, but, of course, most Americans were not rich. Jackson won an overwhelming victory over Clay in the election. Jackson's popularity was national, but in the South he received all the electoral votes except those of South Carolina and Kentucky and some of Maryland's. Even the plantation counties of the southeastern black belt, except for South Carolina, supported Jackson rather than Clay and his American System.

As Americans voted in the presidential election of 1832, South Carolina's long-building resentment against the protective tariff reached a climactic stage, thus confronting President Jackson and the nation with a serious crisis. After nearly a decade of public discussion of the tariff question, most articulate South Carolinians were in agreement in their opposition to protectionism. They disagreed, however, as to what could actually be done about the matter. The Unionists favored trusting traditional procedures and seeking relief through the ballot box and ultimately through congressional action. The States' Rights party, however, advocated quicker and bolder action. Calhoun, who resigned from the vice presidency only to be returned to Washington as one of South Carolina's senators, emerged as the principal leader and chief theoretician of the States' Rightists.

The struggle between the two parties in South Carolina raged fiercely for four years or so before Calhoun and the States' Rights party won a large victory in the legislative elections of 1832. This came about in reaction to a tariff measure that Congress enacted in that year, for while the new bill eliminated some of the "abominations" of the 1828 tariff, it also seemed to indicate a permanent acceptance of the protective principle. Now in control of the legislature, the States' Rightists or Nullifiers proceeded to follow Calhoun's plan, first sketched out in the "Exposition and Protest" of 1828, and called for the election of a convention, the highest expression of the will of the sovereign people. That body, meeting in the state capital, Columbia, in November 1832, voted 136 to 26 in favor of an Ordinance of Nullification which declared the federal tariff laws of 1828 and 1832 "null, void and no law" in

South Carolina, and proceeded to enact an elaborate set of laws to give practical effect to the so-called nullification.

For all of his powers of logic and brilliant constitutional theorizing, Calhoun miscalculated on several aspects of his purportedly peaceful and "legal" plan. Not only did South Carolina's sister southern states emphatically refrain from supporting nullification, but, more important, Andrew Jackson made it abundantly clear that he was bound by the Constitution to see that all federal laws, including even locally unpopular tariffs, were faithfully obeyed. He issued special instructions to federal customs collectors in South Carolina port cities and increased federal military forces in that area.

As the possibility increased of overt conflict between South Carolina and federal authorities, compromisers worked busily in Congress. With Henry Clay playing a prominent role in seeking a compromise solution, and Calhoun lending his support, early in 1833 Congress passed a tariff measure which provided for a gradual reduction in duties over a ten-year period to a level of 20 percent. At the same time, Congress responded favorably to the president's request for special authorization to use federal military forces, if necessary, to protect United States customs officers. Jackson signed both the compromise tariff and the Force Bill—called the "Bloody Bill" in South Carolina—on March 1, 1833.

In South Carolina, the convention which had originally passed the Ordinance of Nullification hastily reassembled. Calhoun traveled from Washington to encourage acceptance of the compromise, and the convention did vote overwhelmingly in favor of rescinding the Ordinance of Nullification. In a rather meaningless, nose-thumbing gesture at Jackson and the federal government, however, the convention passed a new measure nullifying the Force Bill.

The nullification crisis thus ended with several significant results. South Carolina had succeeded in getting the tariff lowered, but Calhoun's theory of nullification proved unacceptable outside South Carolina. Most Georgians disliked the tariff, too, but the legislature of that state declared that "we abhor the doctrine of Nullification as neither a peaceful, nor a constitutional remedy, but, on the contrary, as tending to civil commotion and disunion." Other southern states took a similar stand.

If Calhoun's theory suffered from the episode, Andrew Jackson's stature as a strong champion of the Union rose in much of the nation, including many parts of the South. Some passionate states' rightists in the South joined in attacks on "King Andrew the First," but Jackson had strongly identified himself and the Democracy, as his party was coming to be known, with nationalism or unionism rather than the states' rightist particularism—at least in its nullification aspect—that had captured South Carolina and greatly increased in other southern quarters.

Another fact that the nullification crisis clarified was that the tariff, important though it might be, was not really the sort of issue that deeply stirred human passions and inspired unyielding resistance. It was a pocketbook matter, and, as events demonstrated in 1833, American politicians were richly experienced and adept at compromising such issues. But if the tariff, as an essentially mundane economic matter, was the type of issue that most Americans refused to become too excited about, why had South Carolinians become so aroused and gone originally to such extremes?

South Carolina was a special case. There actually was more on the minds of many of the nullifiers than just the tariff. The state was special in a number of ways, but the most crucial had to do with slavery. Early in the eighteenth century black slaves in the colony of South Carolina outnumbered the white inhabitants, an unprecedented development in Britain's North American colonies. That black majority continued after the Revolution, and South Carolina, alone among the slaveholding states, briefly reopened the African slave trade in the early nineteenth century before the federal government could, under the Constitution's twenty-year compromise, move to prohibit that trade in 1808. Nearly 40,000 Africans were brought into the state, adding an exotic and, according to some white observers, a dangerous element to an already parlous demographic situation. In the low country or tidewater region of the state, where the great plantations produced indigo, sea-island or long-staple cotton, and es-

31

pecially rice, slaves outnumbered whites by majorities ranging from three to one around Charleston to eight to one in the vicinity of Georgetown. During the summer, when malaria forced many of the whites to flee to safer regions, the proportion of blacks became even higher, and absentee ownership compounded various other problems in a slaveholding society.

The cultivated and proud owners of the slaves and plantations of the low country deliberately modeled themselves on the gentry and landed aristocracy of England. But because of slavery, particularly the high proportion of blacks in the population, the South Carolina planters developed deep fears and sensitivities unlike any known in Britain. There were myriad evidences of South Carolinians' morbidity about slavery. During the Missouri crisis, for example, when most southern congressmen refused to defend slavery itself and continued to espouse the Jeffersonian view of slavery as a necessary evil, Senator William Smith of South Carolina, then a bitter foe of Calhoun's nationalist program, berated his fellow southerners for their timidity about slavery and dismissed Jefferson's antislavery views in the *Notes on Virginia* as being "the effusions of the speculative philosophy of his young and ardent mind, and which his riper years have corrected." Smith went on to argue that God's chosen people, the Jews, had both been slaves and later held slaves and that the practice was abundantly sanctioned by the Bible.

Representative Charles Pinckney of South Carolina joined Smith in defending slavery during the Missouri debates and used an argument that would be increasingly heard and centrally important for white southerners in the decades ahead: "The great body of slaves are happier in the present situation than they could be in any other, and the man or men who would attempt to give them freedom, would be their greatest enemies."

Paradoxically, while asserting that the slaves were happy in their bondage, Pinckney and other South Carolinians—indeed, other whites elsewhere in the South—never succeeded in hiding their great fear of slave rebellion. Senator Smith asserted, in fact, that the successfully rebellious slaves of San Domingo in the 1790s had received less provocation than Senator Rufus King of

Massachusetts had provided in his antislavery speeches during the Missouri debates.

Because of South Carolina's historic ties with the West Indies, fearful memories of San Domingo and its great slave uprising were always more prevalent in South Carolina than anywhere else in North America. In 1822, when the shock of the Missouri controversy had barely faded, South Carolina whites found new cause to remember San Domingo and ponder the dangers in their own situation. Authorities in Charleston discovered a plot for a vast slave uprising that had been masterminded by a free black, Denmark Vesey. Inspired by his study of the Bible, the Declaration of Independence, and other political documents—including Senator King's antislavery speeches—Vesey planned one of the most extensive slave insurrections in American history. It was forestalled. Thirty-five of the alleged conspirators were tried and hanged, and thirty-seven others were banished from South Carolina. But white South Carolinians more than ever had to live with their fears.

Pinckney had argued that the slaves were happy. After the Denmark Vesey affair, another South Carolinian candidly took an opposite view and revealed a mind-set that would increasingly, if subtly and indirectly, affect southern politics: "Let it never be forgotten, that 'our NEGROES are truly the *Jacobins* of the country; that they are the *anarchists* and the *domestic enemy*; the *common enemy of civilized society*, and the barbarians who would, IF THEY COULD, become the DESTROYERS of our race.'"

Torn between such fears of the black majority and the oft-repeated clichés about the alleged contentment of the slaves, white South Carolinians in the 1820s found themselves caught up in a never-ending spiral of concern about slavery. In 1824 the Ohio legislature urged Congress and other state legislatures to consider a plan whereby the slaves in the United States might be gradually emancipated, the freed blacks colonized abroad, and the vast expenses of such a scheme borne by the federal government on the grounds that "the evil of slavery is a national one, and that the people and the states of this Union ought mutually to participate in the duties and burthens of removing it."

33

The Ohio plan, soon endorsed by eight northern states, reflected the thinking of the American Colonization Society, which had been launched a few years earlier and had established Liberia on the western coast of Africa as a haven for free blacks from the United States. While moderately antislavery, the Ohio proposal, like the society that pushed it, was also obviously racist in that it assumed that free blacks should not remain in this country. Thomas Jefferson and others had earlier advanced quite similar arguments, although Ohio had added the generous element of the North's helping to pay the costs.

The Ohio initiative received a chilly reception in the South. The South Carolina upper house labelled it "a very strange and ill-advised communication," and the lower house stiffly asserted that "the people of this state will adhere to a system, descended to them from their ancestors, and now inseparably connected with their social and political existence." Governor George M. Troup of Georgia, already embroiled in an angry conflict with President Adams and the federal government about the Indians and their lands in the state, reacted to the Ohio proposal by declaring that "our feelings have been again outraged by officious and impertinent intermeddlings with our domestic concerns." Troup urged his fellow Georgians to be on guard against federal activism, especially concerning slavery, for "the United States' Government, discarding the mask, will openly lend itself to a combination of fanatics for the destruction of every thing valuable in the Southern country; one movement of the Congress unresisted by you, and all is lost."

Nothing came of the Ohio plan, but the alarms and shocks for southern whites concerning slavery abated not a whit. In 1829 authorities in Savannah discovered a pamphlet known as *Walker's Appeal* in the hands of local blacks. Regarded by the whites as dangerously incendiary, the *Appeal* had been written by David Walker, a free black from North Carolina who had moved to Boston. Charging that blacks in America were cruelly mistreated and had been reduced to abject wretchedness by oppressive white masters, Walker urged his fellow blacks to strike for freedom by destroying their masters. "Get the blacks started," Walker declared, "and if you do not have a gang of tigers and lions to deal with, I am a deceiver. . . . let twelve black men get well armed for battle, and they will kill and put to flight fifty whites." Copies of *Walker's Appeal* were soon discovered in South Carolina, Virginia, Louisiana, and elsewhere in the South. White officials, nervous about even public discussion of the sensitive matter, reacted by trying to tighten up on often-ignored laws against teaching slaves to read and write, and new laws were passed restricting the movements and activities of free blacks.

While the scare among whites inspired by *Walker's Appeal* continued, American newspapers in 1830 carried reports of a great debate that had begun in the British Parliament concerning the abolition of slavery in the empire, particularly in the British West Indies. Although the measure was not actually passed until 1833, the British debate added to the growing feeling of isolation and defensiveness felt by many southern slaveholders.

They were not, however, the only Americans to react to the British movement against slavery. The antislavery movement in the United States had been dominated in the first two decades of the nineteenth century by moderates and colonizationists, and many southerners, especially in the upper South, had been included in their ranks. Now, partly as a result of the British debate about slavery, the American antislavery movement took a new direction.

In January 1831, young William Lloyd Garrison in Boston published the first issue of the *Liberator*. Nothing quite like it had been seen in the nation before, and the startled, angry reaction of southerners, who read only the most flamboyant excerpts from the *Liberator* that were widely reprinted in southern newspapers, was immediate and profound. Declaring at the outset that he meant to be "as harsh as truth, and as uncompromising as justice," Garrison denounced moderation and called for immediate abolition of slavery wherever it existed in the United States; if any compensation was to be paid, it should go to those whose liberty had been stolen by wicked, sinful slaveholders. Garrison claimed to be a pacifist, but just as his language was abusive and extreme, so his attitude toward violence was quite ambiguous.

The *Liberator* carried poems about "Afric's sons, uprising from the dust" and bringing "red-handed slaughter" to innocent babes as well as guilty masters. One verse published in July 1831 was designed to be sung by insurrectionary slaves, who were admonished to "strike for God and vengeance now." With a pitifully small number of subscribers, most of them the hard-pressed blacks living in the larger northern cities, the *Liberator* and Garrison quickly became famous because of the publicity given them by angry southern editors.

The southern fury reached new heights when in August 1831 in southeastern Virginia a slave named Nat Turner led an insurrection that resulted in the death of some fifty-five to sixty white persons, mostly women and children. Of the fifty-three blacks subsequently arrested and tried, twenty, including Turner, were hanged, and additional scores of blacks were killed in the panicky aftermath of the insurrection. It was the largest, bloodiest slave rebellion actually to occur in the nineteenth-century South, and had far-reaching and profound repercussions.

Without a scintilla of evidence to prove the point, various prominent southerners immediately jumped to the conclusion that Turner, who was literate and a self-styled preacher, had been inspired by Garrison's *Liberator*. Unwilling to admit that there might simply be an untold number of Nat Turners and Denmark Veseys who so hated slavery that they would fight to destroy the institution, most white southerners took the less painful route of blaming the affair on a "Yankee incendiary" like Garrison or dismissing Turner himself as a deranged fanatic.

In South Carolina the Nat Turner insurrection capped the climax. It came on top of all the various discussions and alarms about slavery that had continued for over a decade—the Missouri crisis, the Denmark Vesey plot, Ohio's emancipation plan, *Walker's Appeal*, the British movement against slavery, and Garrisonian abolitionism. While South Carolina's opposition to the protective tariff had also grown immensely in the 1820s, one inescapable fact about nullification was that it seemed to promise a method whereby South Carolina could protect her slaveholding society should the day ever come when an activist federal government fell into the hands of those who might wish to move against the peculiar institution. Few articulate South Carolinians were willing to discuss their long-range fears about slavery publicly, for the subject was regarded as dangerously sensitive. But a South Carolina newspaper in 1830 came close to making explicit what many other nullifiers were content to leave implicit: "If it is not, it ought to be understood that the Tariff is only one of the subjects of complaint at the South. The Internal Improvement, or general bribery system, and the interference with our domestic policy [i.e., slavery]—most especially the latter—are things which . . . will, if necessary, be met with something more than words." The South Carolina legislature, denouncing any discussion in Congress of the scheme to free and colonize the blacks, declared in 1827: "Should Congress claim the power to discuss and take a vote upon any question connected with domestic slavery . . . it will be neither more nor less than the commencement of a system by which the peculiar policy of South Carolina, upon which is predicated her resources and her prosperity, will be shaken to its foundation."

In South Carolina's confrontation with the federal government in 1832–1833, nullification proved to be an unworkable scheme. Yet that did not mean that those who had championed it had given up the fight. Some of them, according to their opponents, had simply metamorphosed from nullifiers into secessionists. One of the leading Unionists, Benjamin F. Perry, prophetically declared as the crisis ended in 1833: "Nullification is not dead but *sleepeth*. The grand object is disunion, and it will be attempted again."

South Carolina tried nullification in the winter of 1832–1833, but Virginia, in the aftermath of the Nat Turner insurrection, was the scene of a quite different development. While many white Virginians, like other southerners, responded to the insurrection by demanding new laws to repress blacks or stricter enforcement of existing laws, some Virginia leaders suggested that the insurrection merely dramatized the fact that slavery was a dangerous institution and that the danger rose as the proportion of slaves in the total population increased. In Southampton

County, where the Turner insurrection occurred, slaves outnumbered whites three to two. In Virginia east of the Blue Ridge mountains—that is in the piedmont and tidewater—blacks outnumbered whites. If slavery truly was dangerous and possibly harmful to the state, then perhaps consideration should be given to its gradual abolition. The governor and a number of other prominent Virginians so believed.

Early in 1832 a debate began in the Virginia legislature that was the South's most important public discussion of slavery and abolition before the Civil War. It also proved to be one of the last such before the war. Only a few of the champions of abolition argued from the Revolutionary principles of natural rights and equality, for most of them claimed that slavery, in addition to being dangerous, was a drag on Virginia's economic advancement and that it harmed white society in general. Few white Virginians suggested emancipation for the sake of the blacks. The defenders of slavery countered with arguments about the alleged superiority of the existing way of life in Virginia, the happiness of the slaves, and the basic right of private property, including property in slaves.

While there were a handful of opponents of slavery east of the mountains, including Jefferson's grandson and a couple of the most influential newspaper editors in Richmond, most of them came from the western counties, where there were relatively few slaves and a long history of political grievances against the more powerful east. After two weeks of debate, the motion that the legislature should initiate steps looking toward abolition in Virginia was defeated by a vote of 73 to 58. The legislators then contented themselves with voting to try to get the free blacks out of the state and to allow any further action against slavery to "await a more definite development of public opinion." Such a development was indeed shaping up in Virginia and elsewhere in the South, but rather than favoring emancipation, public opinion gradually froze up and consolidated in defense of slavery.

The South, led in this instance by South Carolinians beginning in the 1820s, ceased to view slavery in the long-established manner as a necessary evil. The peculiar institution became, rather, a positive good, the very cornerstone of southern society and life. This development was a tragic one for many reasons, and clearly it was one of the taproots of the Civil War. In the first place, in breaking away from the older, admittedly ambiguous national consensus that slavery where it existed was a necessary evil, the South further isolated and alienated itself from the rest of the nation. Any national action or policy that touched on slavery, either directly or indirectly, would grow more and more difficult to deal with in the decades ahead.

Furthermore, as important an economic interest as slavery represented in the South, the fact remains that the large majority of white southerners owned no slaves. In 1860, for example, over three-fourths of southern whites lived in families that owned no slaves. Of the slaveowning families, about half owned only one to four slaves. Thus slaveholding was in the purely economic interest of a distinct minority of white southerners.

Why then did the white South close ranks in defense of slavery? That is the central question of antebellum southern history, and one that has never been finally answered in a manner that satisfies all parties. Many antislavery spokesmen in the North charged before and during the Civil War that the large slaveholders, despite their distinctly minority status, formed a ruling class that dominated the South. The "lords of the lash," as the large slaveholders were often called in antislavery polemics, were credited not only with control of their communities and states but also with primary responsibility for a whole train of controversial events, from the Mexican War to secession in the winter of 1860–1861. Concerning the latter, for example, Senator Henry Wilson of Massachusetts, a leading antislavery spokesman, made this representative charge: "By means illegitimate and indefensible, reckless of principle and of consequences, a comparatively few men [i.e., the great slaveholders and their agents] succeeded in dragooning whole States into the support of a policy the majority condemned." Wilson and many of his fellow fighters in the antislavery cause believed that the large slaveholders not only formed a dominant ruling class but also were the ringleaders in a series of well planned conspiracies, culminating in secession and war, designed to protect and advance their own interests.

Some influential historians in the last half of the twentieth century have echoed many of the views of Wilson and the other antislavery spokesmen. The historians have generally dropped the conspiracy charge, but they too argue, with considerable sophistication, that the large slaveholders formed a ruling class, an aristocratic or elite group that enjoyed a hegemonic control over the whole of southern life. If white southerners in all classes became fanatic in defense of slavery, these historians maintain, it was because such a policy was in the class interests of the great slaveholders and was successfully carried out by and for them.

An alternative explanation of the South's gradual freezing up in defense of slavery from the 1820s on focuses not on class but on race. The racial dimension of slavery in North America—that is, the fact that black Africans were the slaves of whites of European ancestry—loomed large from the beginning and had always differentiated American slavery from that which had been known in the civilizations of the Greeks, Romans, and others in antiquity.

While the racial aspect of American slavery was always important, not until the nineteenth century did educated Europeans and Americans begin self-consciously to think and write a great deal about the distinct races of mankind. In the eighteenth century, universalist ideas about mankind—such as natural rights allegedly belonging to all men—had prevailed. In the nineteenth century, however, attention shifted markedly to the distinct races of human beings, and inevitably to the allegedly scientifically proven superiority or inferiority of certain races. In the United States the assumption of the superiority of the white race, or, as it was often called, the "Anglo-Saxon" race, over both the Negro and Indian races became a most important fact before and after the Civil War, a fact that massively influenced national politics and policies. And while the Mason-Dixon line came after 1800 to separate the slaveholding states from those states that had eliminated slavery, there was certainly never a Mason-Dixon line for white racism.

Just as whites, South and North, began to think self-consciously about race in the early nineteenth century, so political democracy, as that century defined the term, arrived on the scene at about the same time. There were some exceptions, especially in South Carolina and the other South Atlantic states, but as a result of popular agitation and constitutional reform in the 1820s and 1830s, the advance of political democracy in most of the South matched that of the rest of the nation. By the mid-1830s in Alabama, Mississippi, and Tennessee, government was quite democratic by the standards of that era: the voters, not the legislature, elected the governor; there was universal manhood suffrage (that is, white adult males could vote); the legislatures were based on the white population and were reapportioned regularly; and the voters elected county officials. When Arkansas (1836) and Texas (1845) entered the Union and thus joined the ranks of the slave-holding states, they too had the same democratic features. Three other states in the Deep South—Georgia, Florida (1845), and Louisiana—were not far behind in the advance of political democracy. Neither was Kentucky, except that its county governments continued to be undemocratic.

In the older seaboard states of Maryland, Virginia, North Carolina, and South Caorlina the popular push for democratic reforms had more mixed results. In both Maryland and North Carolina constitutional reforms gave the voters power to elect the governor and moved the basis of apportionment in the legislature in a more democratic direction. In Virginia, while suffrage was broadened, it was still tied to property-holding or taxpaying. And though the traditionally dominant eastern counties in Virginia made concessions to the western ones in the matter of representation in the legislature, the east kept power that was out of proportion to its white population. Both Virginia and South Carolina resisted political reform more than the other southern states: property qualifications for voting and officeholding were kept, county government remained undemocratic, and the legislatures still chose the governors. But despite necessary qualifications, the fact remains that political democracy for white adult males became a reality in most of the South long before the Civil War.

One of the first tangible results of that democratic advance may well have been a more positive and vigorous defense of slavery, for as countless antebellum white southerners as well as later historians have pointed out, slavery was an arrangement of the races as well as a system of labor. By the arrangement, all white persons, no matter how rich or poor they may have been or what social class they may have belonged to, were drastically separated from—and, they believed, kept raised above—the vast majority of the blacks who were slaves. "Break down slavery," one prominent Virginia declared, "and you would with the same blow destroy the great democratic principle of equality among men." He meant, of course, that all whites could allegedly enjoy equality precisely because the blacks were slaves. A Georgian explained that since the black slaves were not citizens, every white who was a citizen felt that he belonged to an elevated class. "It matters not that he is no slaveholder," the Georgian continued, "he is not of the inferior race; he is a freeborn citizen; he engages in no menial occupation. The poorest meets the richest as an equal; sits at his table with him; salutes him as a neighbor; meets him in every public assembly, and stands on the same social platform. Hence there is no war of classes."

There were, despite such assertions as the Georgian's, quite real class tensions among whites, but the argument that there were not was often used by upper-class slaveholders to try to stifle opposition and protect their own interests. Yet nonslaveholding whites also used the argument that all whites were equal, and when they did so they were asserting their hotly claimed superiority to the black slaves.

The classic statement about the racial aspect not only of slavery but of southern history in general was made by historian Ulrich B. Phillips in 1928. In a now-famous essay entitled "The Central Theme of Southern History," Phillips argued that the absolute essence or core of southernism was "a common resolve indomitably maintained" that the South be and always remain "a white man's country." Whether expressed "with the frenzy of a demagogue or maintained with a patrician's quietude," a belief in and adherence to white supremacy was "the cardinal test of a Southerner and the central theme of Southern history." Before the Civil War, the most basic fact about slavery, according to Phillips' interpretation, was that it maintained white supremacy.

Regardless of why the white South gradually closed ranks in defense of slavery—because of the alleged domination of the great slaveholders or, as the evidence increasingly suggests, because of the pride and fears of the race-conscious and politically active nonslaveholding majority—the fact remains that the old necessary-evil concept gave way to the newer and more dynamic idea of slavery as a positive good, and whites of all classes became militant defenders of slavery. An outpouring of speeches and pamphlets in South Carolina beginning in the 1820s marked the beginning of the shift. In the late eighteenth century the Methodist and Baptist leaders in the South had disapproved of slavery, but in 1823 the Reverend Richard Furman, president of the Baptist State Convention in South Carolina, published a biblical defense of slavery. In 1826 the learned Dr. Thomas Cooper, president of South Carolina College (later the University of South Carolina), spoke out in defense of slavery, and in 1829 Governor Stephen Miller of South Carolina asserted: "Slavery is not a national evil; on the contrary, it is a national benefit . . . [and] upon this subject it does not become us to speak in a whisper, betray fear, or feign philanthropy."

That the proslavery argument gained powerful champions in Virginia too became clear in 1832. Having closely followed the slavery debates in the Virginia legislature, Thomas R. Dew, a professor at the College of William and Mary and soon to become its president, published a powerful defense of slavery. Numerous other defenses of slavery continued to appear, right on down to the collapse of the institution in 1865, for the construction and elaboration of the proslavery argument was perhaps the most sustained intellectual activity of the antebellum South. A milestone in the advance of the argument was reached in 1837 when Senator John C. Calhoun, the widely acknowledged possessor of perhaps the keenest political mind in the South, declared on the floor of the United States Senate: "When two races of different origin and distinguished by color, and other physical differences, as well as intellectual [differences] are brought together, the relation now existing in the slave-holding states between the two, is instead of an evil, a good—a positive good." Calhoun and other defenders of slavery usually spoke first and foremost to their fellow white southerners, for lingering doubts about slavery had to be removed and uneasy consciences constantly assuaged.

The attack on the institution from the outside, however, reached new heights in the 1830s. Growing partially out of a religious revival in the North led by Charles G. Finney and partially out of the humanitarian and reforming zeal of certain wealthy New York merchant-philanthropists, the American Anti-Slavery Society was established late in 1833. Although angry northern mobs assailed the abolitionists, who remained unpopular in much of the North until the Civil War, their number did grow. In the mid-1830s they attempted to flood the South with antislavery pamphlets and newspapers, only to inspire mobs in some southern cities to seize the material from the post offices and burn it. In addition, many southern states enacted laws making the distribution of abolitionist literature a felony. Next the Anti-Slavery Society began to flood the United States Congress with petitions demanding the abolition of slavery and the slave trade in the District of Columbia, over which the Constitution gave Congress sole power. Opponents of President Jackson and his Democratic party were happy to see Congress paralyzed as southern congressmen angrily responded to the petitions, and a bitter fight ensued over how the petitions should be handled.

By the late 1830s, however, the American Anti-Slavery Society had fallen into disarray. Not only did the leadership divide over various questions of policy, but the severe economic depression that began in 1837 dried up most of the Society's sources of funds. By the time William Lloyd Garrison and his fellow abolitionists from New England captured control of the organization in 1840, many of the original leaders were turning to the type of political action that the Garrisonians scorned.

For all of the controversy, North and South, that the abolitionists stirred up in the 1830s, they and their cause did not
significantly affect the mainstream of the nation's political life.
The reason for this was that a vigorous two-party system emerged
in the same decade. Since both parties were national in scope and
abolitionism was unpopular in the North and anathema in the
South, the leaders of both parties did their utmost to avoid touch-
ing the slavery question.

The Democrats, galvanized by the bold and therefore controversial leadership of Andrew Jackson, saw their National Republican opponents metamorphose around 1834 into the Whig party.
With a name that recalled British as well as American resistance
to the powers of the Stuart kings and George III, the Whigs were
an amorphous coalition which formed initially to oppose "King
Andrew" and his minions. Despite the fragility of the Whig coalition, for almost two decades the nation witnessed a vigorous
two-party system in operation, and southern voters as much as
those in any other section of the country divided passionately into
Democrats and Whigs.

The southern Whigs were an incredibly mixed lot. The hemp
growers of Kentucky and the great sugar planters of Louisiana
were traditional friends of the protective tariff in the South, and
they gravitated naturally to the support of Clay's American System, which was at the heart of northern Whiggery. Businessmen
in Baltimore, Richmond, and Norfolk tended to be Whigs just
as many had earlier been Federalists and then National Republicans.

The black-belt counties of the South, so-called because of the
fertile dark soil, were, outside of the tidewater, the areas of greatest slaveholding in the South, and these counties were generally
Whig. The claim was sometimes made, in fact, that three-fourths
of the slaves in the South were owned by Whigs. Many of these
planters were Whigs not so much because they liked the whole
American System—though there were parts of it, such as a central bank, which they did support—but because the Whigs presented themselves as champions of order and property and as the
conservative, gentlemanly opponents of the Democratic "rabble."

Some southerners, such as John Tyler of Virginia, became Whigs mainly because they feared and disliked Andrew Jackson's unprecedented display of executive power and the disdain for states' rights that he revealed in the nullification crisis. Southern Whigs were by no means recruited only from the ranks of the larger slaveholders, however. In the North Carolina up-country and in eastern Tennessee, yeoman farmers, who hoped for internal improvements in the form of railways, joined the Whig party. In their eyes, the Whigs were the champions of progress and economic development.

Wildly heterogeneous though the southern Whigs were, they offered the Democrats a vigorous, frequently successful opposition. With both parties claiming nationally to be the true champion of liberty and the people—and each painting the other as a menace to freedom and the Republic—the two southern wings of the parties faced the additional task of assuring the voters that they were solidly behind slavery and the equality of all whites that the peculiar institution allegedly made possible.

Sharing the goal of protecting and promoting liberty and equality for whites, Whigs and Democrats differed as to the best way of achieving those goals. There were numerous variations and issues from state to state, but generally the Whigs favored a positive role for government in encouraging economic development and therefore economic opportunities for all. The Democrats, on the other hand, opposed federal or state financing of internal improvements such as railroads or canals on the grounds that such policies aided the rich and powerful few at the ultimate expense of the impoverished masses and that public debt, the inevitable by-product of an activist role for the government, would lead to corruption. With Democrats stressing the government's obligation merely to protect the equal rights of all white men, Whigs looked less fearfully upon government and the help it might give to the capitalistic market economy.

In an Upper South state such as North Carolina, where historian Marc Kruman has carefully studied the workings of the second party system, the Whigs took the lead in having the state government aid in financing major railroads and in launching banks for which the state provided a minority share of the capital. Tar Heel Democrats bitterly opposed such measures on the grounds that they favored special interests and threatened liberty and equality.

Studying Alabama in the Deep South, historian J. Mills Thornton III likewise argues that Whigs there maintained that positive state action would benefit society as a whole while the Democrats feared any increase of power in government or in such private institutions as state-chartered corporations. Fierce political battles raged in Alabama about a host of issues ranging from banking to the removal of the Creek Indians, but Thornton suggests that there was actually only one issue in the state's politics: how to protect liberty and white equality, or, to put the matter another way, how to avoid slavery. While this same republican ideology, the legacy of the American Revolution, animated northerners as well as southerners, the presence of large numbers of black slaves in the South served as a constant reminder to southern whites of the grim reality that lay behind the politicians' rhetoric.

Whether in the Upper or the Deep South, both parties claimed to be staunch defenders of slavery. Each party, in fact, claimed superiority in that respect and attempted to arouse suspicion among the voters as to the soundness or trustworthiness of the opposition in championing "southern rights." Paradoxically, by constantly stressing the centrality of southern rights and the alleged threats to the institution of slavery from various northern groups, the state political parties actually increased southern sectional sensitivity at the same time that the national parties worked to lessen the dangers of sectionalism.

As a two-party region, moreover, the South and its interests were important to both parties. The paradox was that the South's political sectionalism actually diminished in the very same period in which its feelings about and defense of the peculiar institution moved farther and farther from the older national consensus about slavery. That is, although political sectionalism waned, the South's cultural sectionalism increased. But as long as the national leaders of both parties scrupulously avoided offending the South on the slavery question, the region seemed well integrated into the nation's vigorous and often clamorous political life.

Avoiding, or at least containing, the slavery issue was not easy. It came up in 1836 when the Texans successfully rebelled against Mexico, declared their independence, and sought to be annexed by the United States. The Texans' desire to have slaves had been one of the sources of their trouble with the Mexican government, and that same matter of slavery in Texas made some northerners hostile to the idea of annexation, especially if it should involve a war with Mexico. John Quincy Adams, for example, had returned to the national scene as a member of the House of Representatives from Massachusetts, and strongly opposed the annexation of additional slaveholding territory. Calhoun and his allies, on the other hand, warmly welcomed the prospect of a slaveholding Texas. Other southern leaders felt more cautious about Texas and refused to support Calhoun.

Since the matter was divisive and 1836 a presidential-election year, Jackson, who privately favored annexation, advised delay. After Britain extended recognition to the Republic of Texas, the United States did likewise, and Jackson passed the problem on to his hand-picked successor, Martin Van Buren. Despite repeated requests for annexation from the Texans and pressure from Calhoun and some other southerners and westerners, President Van Buren also feared the possible repercussions, both domestic and Mexican, of such a step, and refused to act.

Seriously handicapped by the severe depression that had begun in 1837, Van Buren and the Democrats were beaten in 1840 by the Whigs. Though still so mixed and fragile a coalition that they could not come up with a platform, the Whigs had learned some shrewd political tricks: following the Democratic example of 1828, they selected a military hero from the War of 1812, William Henry Harrison of Ohio, as their presidential candidate. They teamed him up with a states' rights Whig from Virginia, John Tyler, as the vice presidential nominee, and conducted a noisy, silly campaign—mostly torchlight parades and barbecues—that won them the election. In the South, the Whigs carried seven states and lost only Virginia, South Carolina, Alabama, and Arkansas to the Democrats.

Whig luck ran out quickly. One month after he took office, Harrison died. John Tyler thus became president and, to the horror of Henry Clay and other Whigs who had so long railed against Jackson's use of the veto power, Tyler, or "His Accidency" as his foes dubbed him, proceeded to veto one after another of the measures that Clay and his friends pushed through Congress, such as bills to raise the tariff and to create a new central bank.

As these political dramas titillated the nation in the early 1840s, the Texas question heated up. Annoyed by the United States' refusal to act, Sam Houston, president of the Republic of Texas, began to flirt with Britain. Rumors soon circulated in Washington, and then through the country, that Texas would enter an alliance with cotton-hungry Britain and that British abolitionists might try to help end slavery in Texas. President Tyler, alienated from Clay and the main body of the Whigs, responded to growing concern about Texas among both southerners and westerners by negotiating a treaty of annexation with the Texan government. Calhoun, whom Tyler named as secretary of state in 1844, gave the whole matter a highly sectional and proslavery coloration when he argued publicly that the treaty was essential to protect slavery in the southern states and in Texas.

John Quincy Adams and twelve other members of the House of Representatives, mostly antislavery or "Conscience" Whigs, had earlier issued an address warning against an alleged conspiracy to bring more slave territory into the Union. They charged that the plot represented an "attempt to eternize an institution and a power of nature so unjust in themselves, so injurious to the interests and abhorrent to the feelings of the people of the free states, as in our opinion not only inevitably to result in a dissolution of the Union, but fully to justify it." Given such strong feelings on the part of some, but by no means all, northerners, the fact that Tyler's treaty failed to be ratified by the Senate is hardly surprising. And Whig animosity against Tyler was such that every southern Whig senator, save one, voted against the treaty. Tyler had, however, succeeded in forcing the Texas question to the front and center of the nation's political stage.

Such a prominent place for the Texas question was exactly what Van Buren and Clay did not want. Those two veteran leaders fully expected to be the presidential nominees of their respective parties in 1844, and both hoped to avoid the explosive question by opposing immediate annexation. They were bucking extremely strong headwinds, however, for the prospect of territorial expansion excited a growing number of Americans in the 1840s.

Southern and western Democrats made themselves the special champions of the nation's "manifest destiny" to expand. When the Democratic national convention met in 1844, the delegates, recalling vague claims to Texas as part of the Louisiana Purchase and ignoring a United States treaty with Spain in 1819, demanded the "reannexation of Texas." To balance Texas, however, the Democrats called for "the reoccupation of Oregon," that is, for an end to the joint occupation with the British of that territory in the Pacific Northwest. In addition to these territorial planks, the Democrats called for a lowering of the tariff and the establishment of an independent treasury to divorce public money from private banking. Passing over Van Buren, who had balked on Texas, the Democrats chose as their presidential candidate James K. Polk of Tennessee, a staunch Jacksonian who had served as Speaker of the House of Representatives and governor of Tennessee. As expected, Clay won the Whig nomination and, though he tried to straddle the fence on the Texas question, he and his party declared for the familiar programs of the American System.

Polk and the Democrats won, but the election was extremely close. The southern states gave Polk 60 of their 104 electoral votes, with Clay winning only in Maryland, North Carolina, Kentucky, and Tennessee. But the Whigs showed considerable strength even in those states that the Democrats carried, and the returns do not suggest anything like solid southern support for expansionism. The election was so close in the nation at large that Polk's narrow margin of victory in New York state gave him the presidency. That happened partly because in 1844 the Liberty party, the nation's first antislavery political party, took enough votes away from Henry Clay to throw New York into the Democratic column. The Liberty party had first appeared in the 1840 election, and though it then polled only a little more than 7,000 votes, in 1844 it won 62,300.

With Polk elected but not yet inaugurated, President Tyler made another move to gain Texas. Interpreting the Democratic victory as a national mandate for territorial expansion, he abandoned the idea of a treaty of annexation and urged Congress to admit Texas into the Union by a joint resolution, which would require only a simple majority. Northern Whigs bitterly protested, but enough southern Whigs joined with the Democrats for Tyler's plan to succeed. As far as the United States and Texas were concerned, though not in Mexico's eyes, the annexation of Texas was an accomplished fact before Polk actually took office.

Neither Polk nor countless other Americans wanted merely Texas from the vast, shakily-controlled northern part of Mexico. Within days of his inauguration, Polk acknowledged that he meant somehow to acquire California in addition to getting the tariff reduced, the independent treasury established, and the Oregon boundary matter settled. The last three goals he and his supporters in Congress achieved impressively, though some of his northern critics charged that in the peaceful settlement of the Oregon matter the United States gained less territory than it should have. In pursuit of California, however, Polk led the nation into a war with Mexico, and from that came a sectional crisis that threatened, for a while at least, to destroy the Union.

❧

From Sectional Crisis
to the Eve of Disunion
1846–1860

CONTRARY TO CHARGES made by northern antislavery leaders at the time and echoed by various historians since, "the South" did not clamor for war with Mexico. Southerners were not of a single mind about the war or the acquisition of new territory. Calhoun, along with many—probably most—other southerners, had strongly supported the annexation of Texas, but Calhoun and numerous others in the South opposed war with Mexico for a variety of reasons. John A. Campbell of Alabama, one of Calhoun's correspondents and later a justice of the United States Supreme Court, argued that in the long run the acquisition of Mexico's northern lands would work against the interests of the South. Why? Because, Campbell believed, whether correctly or incorrectly, the lands in question were not suitable for slavery, and incorporating them into the United States would lead to "an increase of the strength of the nonslaveholding states and a corresponding diminution of our own."

Despite this southern opposition to the war and skepticism about its purposes, the fact remained that Polk was a southern Democrat, albeit one very much in the Jacksonian mold, and most southern Democrats supported him and his policies even if Calhoun and many southern Whigs did not. Northern Whigs, especially John Quincy Adams and his antislavery allies among the Conscience Whigs, kept up a loud drumbeat of charges that the war had been plotted by slaveholders and had as its great purpose the acquisition of future slave states.

Such charges were embarrassing to northern Democrats who supported both Polk and the war. When a bill appropriating funds with which Polk hoped to buy California and New Mexico, and thus end the war, reached the House in August 1846, Representative David Wilmot, a Democrat from Pennsylvania, offered a fateful amendment. Carefully using language borrowed from the Northwest Ordinance of 1787, language which was originally that of Thomas Jefferson, Wilmot proposed that "as an express and fundamental condition to the acquisition of any territory from the Republic of Mexico . . . neither slavery nor involuntary servitude shall ever exist in any part of said territory, except for crime, whereof the party shall first be duly convicted." The Wilmot Proviso did not apply to Texas, for it had already been admitted as a slaveholding state before the Mexican War began. Since the principal ideas involved in the fight about the Proviso would dominate the politics of the 1850s, they are worth a careful examination.

The response to David Wilmot's call for federal prohibition of slavery in any territory that might be gained from Mexico was electrifying, first in Congress and ultimately throughout the nation. In the House of Representatives party lines were almost totally shattered, as southern Whigs and southern Democrats voted against the Proviso only to be outvoted by the northern members of both parties. Although the measure failed in the Senate, it was later reintroduced, repassed in the House, and debated with increasing intensity and rancor both in Congress and in the nation at large throughout the Mexican War and afterwards. Just as northern newspapers and state legislatures endorsed the federal ban on slavery's extension, southerners protested and threatened with rising vehemence. In a sense, the showdown between North and South on the Proviso was merely postponed until after the war with Mexico had ended and a new president had been elected in 1848. But in August 1846 a Boston newspaper prophetically and accurately observed of Representative Wilmot's amendment: "As if by magic, it brought to a head the great question which is about to divide the American people."

The explanation of why northerners and southerners reacted

as they did to the Proviso also sheds light on why Wilmot's proposal immediately and profoundly affected the mainstream of the
nation's political life in a way that abolitionism had never done.
Perhaps it was paradoxical, but the diluted antislavery of Wilmot's call for a federal ban on slavery in the territories, which
also came to be known as the free soil idea, packed a great deal
more political dynamite than all of the fulminations against slavery of William Lloyd Garrison and other abolitionists.

The North's reasons for supporting the Wilmot Proviso were
numerous and quite mixed, but at least three substantial facts
might be noted. In the first place, the nation had earlier acted to
bar the extension of slavery in certain areas, first in the Northwest
Ordinance of 1787 and again in 1820 in the Missouri Compromise. The constitutional propriety of those actions had not been
significantly questioned when they were taken, and most northerners saw no reason to raise any constitutional question in 1846.
Garrisonians denounced the Constitution as a "wicked pact with
the Devil" because it sanctioned slavery in the states, and Garrison's demands that the northern states dissolve the Union in order
to escape the link with sinful slaveholders were dramatically ac-
companied on occasion by his literally burning a copy of the Constitution. Such ideas and actions shocked and outraged the vast
majority of northerners. They were obviously more comfortable
with the Proviso from the standpoint of the Constitution and history.

Secondly, while most northerners were clearly opposed to abolitionism, they had always been uneasy about and often hostile to
the spread of slavery. That had been demonstrated repeatedly, not
only in 1787 and 1820, but on numerous less famous occasions.
That hostility arose partly from a questioning of slavery itself—
whether from humanitarian, moral, or ideological reasons—and
partly from purely sectional politics involving such matters as the
three-fifths compromise and the political power of the sections in
Congress and the electoral college. As for slavery where it already
existed, that is, in the southern states, there is no evidence that
the majority of northerners in the middle of the nineteenth century had moved far beyond the old national consensus, with all of

its ambiguities and contradictions: they still regarded slavery there as a necessary evil. But the territories, the West, were another matter.

A third factor behind the northern popularity of Wilmot's call for territorial free soil through federal fiat was that the idea and the movement that soon grew around it were packed with racial ambiguities. Wilmot himself declared that his purpose in the Proviso was to preserve the territories for "the sons of toil, of my own race and own color." In other words, it was very much a white man's proviso, and many racist northerners, who were indifferent to or even opposed to abolitionism, could support such a demand for free soil. The antislavery movement thus acquired a complexity and ambiguity that would continue and would help to account for its increasing political potency in the North.

Southern reasons for opposing the Wilmot Proviso were no less complicated than the northern reasons for supporting it. The intensity of the South's reaction against the proposal was, first of all, the clearest evidence of what the proslavery movement had accomplished in the South since the 1820s. If slavery was a positive good, as southerners had been so obsessively telling themselves for two decades or so, how could the south possibly agree to have the institution stigmatized by federal prohibition of its introduction into the territories? To agree to such a northern-inspired ban would be to deny the South's equality in the nation, and that both slaveholders and the nonslaveholding majority were adamantly unwilling to do. Many southerners now began to argue that a federal ban on slavery in the territories would be but the first step toward federal moves against slavery in the states. That, above all, the white South was not about to tolerate.

Another manifestation of changes that had occurred in the South's thinking about slavery and all that related to it had to do with the constitutionality of federal prohibition of slavery in the territories. When the Missouri Compromise banned slavery north of the 36° 30' parallel in the Louisiana Purchase Territory, only a few southerners raised constitutional objections. Yet in the late 1840s the belief that the Constitution gave the federal government no power to prohibit slavery in the territories became a key southern dogma. Calhoun gave the clearest formulation of the southern position, and while he failed in most of his efforts to unify the South politically, on this particular point he achieved great success.

The Calhounian argument, which became the South's in this case, was that 1) the territories belonged to the states as co-owners; 2) citizens of any one state had the same rights under the Constitution as citizens of other states to take their property, including slave property, into the commonly owned territories; and 3) any federal law contrary to the above would be in clear violation of the Constitution. In making this argument, it should be noted, Calhoun and the South were insisting that there was nothing different or special about slave property, and that too was a change from the view that had earlier prevailed in the South. Calhoun eventually carried the argument even further, and the great majority of southerners refused at that time to accept his more extreme refinements of the matter. But on the matter of the Wilmot Proviso's alleged unconstitutionality the political South achieved a remarkable degree of unity.

As to whether southerners seriously believed that future slave states could be made out of California and New Mexico, the evidence is mixed and contradictory. As mentioned earlier, John A. Campbell of Tennessee believed the lands were unsuitable for slavery. Henry Clay and numerous other southerners repeatedly said the same thing. Were southerners objecting to the Proviso not because they envisioned future slave states in the region involved but as a first line of defense against a federal stigmatization of and eventual moves against slavery itself? The whole matter became more complicated by later, unforeseen developments in California, as will be seen. Suffice it to say that just as opinions about the possibility of slavery's entering the region differed sharply at the time, so have they continued to differ among historians.

The territories about which Americans became so angrily divided were officially ceded by Mexico when the war ended in 1848. The war also provided a new president, for the Whigs replayed in that same year their tactic of nominating a popular military hero. General Zachary Taylor had led the victorious American army at the battle of Buena Vista; he was a Louisiana slaveholder who had had no experience or interest in politics. Neither he nor the party that nominated him took a stand on the territorial question, but his record in the victorious war made him "available" to the Whigs and irresistible also to the majority of American voters. The Democrats nominated Lewis Cass of Michigan, who tried to escape the territorial dilemma by suggesting that Congress remain silent about slavery and let the actual settlers who went into the territories decide the matter. The Liberty party gave way to a larger, all-northern Free Soil party which, as its name implied, championed the Proviso and named Martin Van Buren as its candidate. Taylor carried seven southern states, but the thousands of southerners who voted for him were in for a surprise. He turned out to be an interesting example of the fact that neither geography nor slaveholding necessarily determined a person's politics, even in an increasingly sectionalized nation.

At the same time Taylor was being elected president, California was the scene of a spectacular gold rush. The metal was discovered there in January 1848, and the people who rushed to share in the bonanza from all over the United States—as well as from other parts of the globe—did not have slavery on their minds. They soon needed a territorial government, for as someone observed, the wild and woolly situation constituted a state of nature that would have made a Tory out of Rousseau. Congress, however, remained bitterly paralyzed by the sectional battle about slavery in the territories.

The continued existence of national political parties, battered though they were by the winds of both northern and southern sectionalism, proved the saving factor in the crisis. Both parties were badly shaken, the Whigs clearly more so than the Democrats. But the organizations at least existed, and there were yet some leaders who tried to transcend sectional verities and alleged moral absolutes in order to hold the nation together.

The varied southern response to Calhoun's efforts to unify the South offered one important illustration of the continued importance of party ties. Calhoun and his allies among the southern Democrats were more alarmed than ever by the South's minority status in the Union. Sectional equality in the Senate was clearly momentary, for numerous free states would eventually be carved out of the territory north of the Missouri Compromise line. In the House of Representatives and in the electoral college the northern majority that had existed even before 1820 had grown much larger. Behind such developments also lay the fact that great tides of immigrants from Ireland, Britain, Germany, and elsewhere were pouring into the North while only a handful entered the South.

In the light of such demographic and geographical facts and because of the enthusiastic northern response to the Wilmot Proviso, Calhoun believed that only a politically unified South had any hope of protecting its vital interests and remaining in the Union with security. With part of his argument Calhoun had considerable success: the great majority of southerners, whether Whig or Democrat, seemed to agree that federal prohibition of slavery in the territories was not sanctioned by the Constitution. But Calhoun pushed the argument further. Ever the logician, even if common sense had to be sacrificed, he argued that the federal government had an obligation in the territories to give protection to all property, including slaves, during the territorial stage. Just as the supporters of the Wilmot Proviso insisted on a positive prohibition of slavery, so Calhoun went 180 degrees in the opposite direction and demanded federal protection for it.

Such extremism and logic-chopping proved too much for even some southern Democrats, and most southern Whigs were not about to follow Calhoun so far. His friends called a caucus of all southern congressmen early in 1849 and sought their signatures on an address that contained the demand for federal protection of slavery in the territories, along with various other southern concerns. Out of 121 southern congressmen, 73 refused to sign, and only 2 of the 48 southern Whigs would sign. Clearly, sectionalism had not obliterated party ties.

Despite the obvious unwillingness of many southerners to unite behind Calhoun and his program, the prolonged crisis that had begun in 1846 clearly inspired at least thoughts of drastic action in the minds of a growing number of southerners, who reacted to northern charges and threats. While the great bulk of the Wilmot Proviso's backers were not abolitionists, they nevertheless adopted the same moral passion and verbal extremism as the older group. An Ohio congressman, for example, warned the South: "We will establish a cordon of free states that shall surround you; and then we will light up the fires of liberty on every side until they melt your present chains and render all your people free." Enraged by such talk and frightened by the northern majority in the House, some southerners began talking openly of disunion, the secession of the southern states, as their only safe and honorable recourse.

States' rights sentiment had grown sporadically in the South since about 1820. In the fights about the protective tariff, Indian policy, and even the Bank of the United States, many southerners had grown familiar and comfortable with the argument that the Constitution was a compact between sovereign states, that the federal government based on the Constitution was but the agent of those states, and that, in the last analysis, not the agent but the sovereign states had the power to judge the constitutional propriety of federal actions. Calhoun's nullification plan had been built on such thinking but had proved a failure in action. In the late 1840s a growing minority of southerners, faced with the possibility of a northern majority's enactment of what so many southerners saw as an unconstitutional insult in the Wilmot Proviso, talked not of nullification but of secession. A group of Calhoun's supporters gathered in Mississippi in October 1849 and issued a call for the southern states to send delegates to a convention to be held in Nashville, Tennessee, in June 1850. The clear implication was that if the new Congress that was to assemble in December 1849 and the new Whig president, Zachary Taylor, acted on the central question of slavery in the territories in a manner considered hostile to the South, then the southern states would use the Nashville convention as a starting point for drastic action.

When the new Congress met it was so paralyzed by sectional animosities that it could do nothing at first. The House of Representatives could not even organize itself and elect a Speaker, for neither Whigs nor Democrats held a clear majority, and the presence of ten Free Soilers further complicated the situation. For nearly three weeks the House was filled with acrimonious charges and countercharges. The seriousness of the sectional crisis was perhaps best indicated when Representative Robert Toombs of Georgia, a distinguished Southern Whig, declared to the northern majority: "I do not hesitate to avow before this House and the Country, and in the presence of the living God, that if, by your legislation, you seek to drive us from the territories of California and New Mexico, purchased by the common blood and treasure of the whole people, and to abolish slavery in this District [of Columbia], thereby attempting to fix a national degradation upon half the states of this Confederacy, *I am for disunion*."

The House finally elected a Speaker, but President Taylor, for one, refused to take seriously the threat posed by even such a leading southern Whig as Toombs. Politically naive and inexperienced, Taylor put himself largely under the influence of Senator William H. Seward of New York, one of the most prominent and outspoken of the antislavery Conscience Whigs. Soon the southern-born president was assuring northern audiences that slavery was not to be further extended. He advised Toombs that if Congress should pass the Wilmot Proviso, he would not veto it.

Meanwhile, the Californians proceeded to draw up a state constitution, one making no provision for slavery, and to apply directly for statehood. California would thus bypass the controversial territorial stage and become a free state. In Taylor's message to Congress, he recommended that Congress act favorably on the Californians' request and suggested that New Mexico too "at no very distant period" might follow the same route. Taylor's plan, as southerners quickly saw and fiercely resented, would exclude slavery from the Southwest just as effectively as the Wilmot Proviso would have. Southern fury at the president, who had come to be regarded in his native region as a renegade and traitor, knew no bounds.

Even such veteran national Whig leaders as Senators Henry

Clay and Daniel Webster believed that the president was blindly ignoring the depth of southern anger and the danger of disunion. The veteran Kentuckian, famed for his key role in effecting important compromises in 1820 and 1833, prepared once again to take the lead in seeking a compromise that he hoped would end the crisis and preserve the Union. Determined to focus the attention first of Congress and then of the nation on the specific, concrete issues, Clay hoped to avoid the large abstract principles concerning the right and wrong of slavery that had so divided the nation. In measures dealing with the major sources of sectional tension, Clay proposed 1) that the federal government remain silent concerning slavery in California and admit it to the Union with the constitution preferred by Californians, that is, as a free state; 2) that the federal government also remain silent concerning slavery in the remainder of the Mexican Cession (the New Mexico and Utah territories) and allow the settlers who went there to decide the matter for themselves; 3) that the bitterly disputed boundary between the state of Texas and the New Mexico Territory be settled largely in favor of the latter, with the federal government to compensate Texas by taking over its public debt; 4) that the slave trade be abolished in the District of Columbia but that slavery there be reaffirmed and not ended unless both Maryland and the people of the District agreed to end it; and 5) that a new fugitive slave law be enacted to enforce more satisfactorily to the South the provision in the Constitution which stipulated that a person "held to Service or Labour in one state . . . escaping into another . . . shall be delivered upon Claim of the party to whom such Service or Labour may be due."

Henry Clay's proposals set the stage for one of the most famous and dramatic Senate debates in United States history. With President Taylor and his allies obstructing the efforts at compromise, Calhoun, who came from his sick-bed to have his speech read for him by a colleague, warned in effect that the proposals were inadequate to deal with the danger to the Union from the South's apprehensions about the antislavery movement and that nothing less than a regional veto power would ensure the South's safety in the Union. Webster, defying the strong sentiment for the Wilmot Proviso in his native New England, lent his support to Clay's proposals, while Seward's phrase that there was "a higher law than the Constitution" was one that southerners especially would long remember and denounce.

As the great debate continued in Washington, the Southern Convention, which had been intended to speak for a united South, assembled in Nashville in June 1850 and proved to be something of a dud. Calhoun had died several weeks earlier, but the most important fact affecting the convention was that Congress seemed to be at least on the road to compromise. Six states—North Carolina, Louisiana, and border states of Delaware, Maryland, Kentucky, and Missouri—sent no delegates to the convention. Only five of the nine states that were represented sent official, formally named delegates. Thus, instead of presenting a united southern front, the convention dramatized the fact that, while southerners of all persuasions were determined to protect slavery, they strongly disagreed as to how that should be done. A minority known as the ultra-states' rightists, or fire-eaters, saw secession and the formation of a separate southern nation as the only hope of safety for the South and its peculiar institution. Robert B. Rhett of South Carolina, Edmund Ruffin of Virginia, and William L. Yancey of Alabama were among the leading fire-eaters. A substantial majority of southerners, however, refused to abandon hope for safety within the Union and frowned on the idea of secession as impracticable or dangerous. With the hope of compromise in the offing, the great majority of southerners looked not to the Nashville convention, which achieved little or nothing of importance, but to the United States Congress.

President Taylor's sudden death in July 1850 removed one major obstacle to compromise, but the omnibus compromise measure fell victim to its foes on both ends of the spectrum and failed to pass. With the seventy-three-year-old Clay exhausted and temporarily out of the battle, a vigorous young Democrat from Illinois, Senator Stephen A. Douglas, assumed command of the compromise forces. With strong support from the new president, Millard Fillmore of New York, Douglas separated the omnibus measure into several separate bills and through adroit politicking and the masterly combining of voting blocs managed to get them all passed by September.

The great majority in the South, as in the North, were greatly relieved and satisfied by what came to be known immediately as the Compromise of 1850. There were, to be sure, ambiguities in the way in which the new laws were enacted despite the fact that northern and southern majorities in Congress had continued to oppose each other; and there were unclarities about the popular sovereignty feature of the New Mexico-Utah measure. But the great majority of political leaders and voters refused to worry over those seemingly small points and instead celebrated what they hoped was the end of the explosively divisive matter of slavery in the territories.

There were important minorities in both sections who did not like the compromise. In the South, the secessionist fire-eaters felt that their states had missed a golden opportunity to escape from a Union which they regarded as humiliating and dangerous to their section. The compromise measures they believed were totally inadequate and unfair to the South. One fire-eating South Carolina editor put the matter starkly: "We must give up the Union or give up slavery." In the North, since the Garrisonian abolitionists scorned all political action as well as the Union itself, their hostility or indifference to the compromise surprised no one, but the continued opposition of such veteran northern Whigs and supporters of the Wilmot Proviso as Senator Seward did not augur well for the national future of the Whig party.

Despite the dissenting minorities of both sections, the "finality" of the compromise became the political watchword and slogan of the day. In much of the South, with Georgia leading the way, national party lines were temporarily forgotten as those who supported the compromise and called themselves Unionists squared off against the more secession-minded Southern Rights party. In one state after another, except South Carolina, the Unionists won substantial victories. The southern Unionists made clear, however, that their support for compromise and the Union was conditional on the alleged rights of the South, particularly concerning slavery, being recognized and upheld by the nation. The new

Fugitive Slave Law, for example, was singled out as a concrete test, and it was one about which trouble was not long in coming. Although relatively few slaves were actually recovered under the law, its great unpopularity in the North meant that it continued to be a source of bitter sectional controversy.

The nation thus survived the sectional crisis that raged from 1846 into 1850, but one important political institution, the Whig party, was mortally wounded during the long battle. Just how deep and unbridgeable were the divisions between the southern and northern Whigs became clear in the presidential election of 1852. The southern Whigs wished to have the party endorse the compromise and nominate President Fillmore, who had played a key role in its enactment, to succeed himself. Northern Whigs, with Seward and editor Horace Greeley of the strongly antislavery *New York Tribune* prominent in their ranks, championed another hero of the Mexican War, General Winfield Scott of Virginia, and were by no means eager to endorse the finality of the compromise. Heavily sectional voting gave the southern Whigs their way on the platform, but northern Whigs managed to have Scott named as the party's presidential candidate.

With bitter memories of Seward's influence over an earlier southern-born military hero, the southern Whigs deserted the party's nominee in droves. Robert Toombs spoke for many when he declared: "We can never have peace and security with Seward, Greeley and Co. in the ascendant in our national counsels, and we had better purchase them by the destruction of the Whig party than of the Union. If the Whig party is incapable of rising to the same standard of nationality as the motley crew which opposes it under the name of the Democracy, it is entitled to no resurrection. It will have none."

Given the disharmony among the Whigs, the victory of the Democratic presidential candidate, Franklin Pierce of New Hampshire, in 1852 surprised few. He and his party were firmly committed to the finality of the compromise as well as to keeping the slavery question out of the political arena. Pierce's lop-sided victory in the electoral vote—254 to 42—concealed several important facts, however. In the North he did not receive a majority of the popular vote. And in the South, although Scott carried only Tennessee and Kentucky, and the national Whig party was disintegrating, the state and local Whig organizations remained alive and competitive. Thus, although southern Whigs increasingly found themselves adrift in national politics, locally they continued to fight the Democrats as vigorously as ever. The South was far from being politically unified or dominated by one party, but the early 1850s did bring relative tranquility on the political front and marked economic prosperity. While the prosperity continued, the finality of the compromise and the tranquility ended abruptly and explosively in 1854.

The last person in the world who would have wished deliberately to reopen the sectional battle about slavery was Senator Stephen Douglas. One of the chief architects of the Compromise of 1850, his abilities, ambitions, and national outlook made him a strong presidential possibility. Yet it was Douglas who introduced, fought for, and finally helped to pass the Kansas-Nebraska Act. The ensuing political storm wrecked not only his career but ultimately the nation.

Douglas originally had railroads rather than slavery on his mind when he began with the matter. An early and important champion of the much-discussed transcontinental railway to the Pacific, he was also chairman of the Senate Committee on Territories, and understandably a strong booster of Chicago and indeed the whole midwestern and western region. While southerners were pushing hard to have the Pacific railway built in their part of the country, Douglas and others worked assiduously to promote a northern or midwestern route. To facilitate that route, they wanted to secure territorial government for the region west of Iowa and Missouri. Since the area lay north of the 36° 30′ parallel in the Louisiana Purchase, slavery had been barred there under the Missouri Compromise of 1820.

Douglas had tried before to get a Nebraska Territorial bill through Congress but had failed, partly because southern congressmen objected to the slavery ban. As the fight about the Wilmot Proviso had revealed, they had come to regard such a ban as both unconstitutional and unfair to the South. Many northerners, of course, sharply disagreed. In 1854 Douglas at first intended simply to incorporate into his Nebraska bill the language concerning slavery that had been used in the New Mexico-Utah legislation of 1850: that "when admitted as a State or States, the said territory . . . shall be received into the Union, with or without slavery, as their constitution may prescribe at the time of their admission." There was to be no explicit mention of the Missouri Compromise, and Douglas appeared to assume that he could finesse that troublesome matter and have the popular-sovereignty formula simply supersede the older ban on slavery in the territory.

Certain southern senators, particularly David Atchison, a Missouri Democrat, and Archibald Dixon, a Kentucky Whig, felt strongly that repeal of the Missouri Compromise by inference, if that was what Douglas intended, was totally inadequate and that if Douglas wanted their support for his bill he would have to include an explicit repeal of the Missouri Compromise. After considerable negotiation and discussion, Douglas, yielding to Dixon's argument, declared: "By God, Sir, you are right. I will incorporate [the repeal] in my bill, though I know it will raise a hell of a storm."

Douglas probably did not realize just how much of a "hell of a storm" the repeal of the thirty-four-year-old ban on slavery would inspire. A sensational address issued by Senators Salmon P. Chase of Ohio and Charles Sumner of Massachusetts, together with other antislavery leaders in Congress, charged Douglas in the purplest of prose with being a moral monster and a villainous puppet of southern slaveholders. His territorial measure, which had finally become the Kansas-Nebraska bill, was, according to the antislavery leaders, part and parcel of a sinister conspiracy to transform those territories eventually into slave states.

Actually Douglas intended no such thing. He believed that, with popular sovereignty and its corollary of federal silence on the issue of slavery in the territories, the West could be won for free soil while the nation avoided a dangerously divisive issue. He was fully aware of the geography and climate of the West and of the great tides of immigration and migration that favored the

North. He had declared in 1850, for example: "We have a vast territory, stretching from the Mississippi to the Pacific, which is rapidly filling up with a hardy, enterprising, and industrious population, large enough to form at least seventeen new free states. . . . I think I am safe in assuming that each of these will be free territories and free states, whether Congress shall prohibit slavery or not." Such views became obscured or even overlooked in the stormy controversy about the Kansas-Nebraska bill and the unprecedentedly bitter charges that the antislavery leaders hurled at Douglas. In the last analysis, it would be his personal fate to be a nationally oriented leader at a time when the easier road to political success and power in both North and South was a sectional one. Douglas hoped for federal silence on the issue of slavery in the territories. When impassioned sectionalists in the South as in the North came to believe that they had God and Truth on their respective side and that the federal government neither could nor should remain silent on the slavery issue, there would be no room left for Douglas or his middle ground of popular sovereignty.

That development lay in the future, however, and in 1854 Douglas gained considerable support from the South. Initially most southern congressmen were taken by surprise by the furor about the Kansas-Nebraska measure. Several, such as Senator Sam Houston from Texas, spoke out strongly against the measure, and most agreed that slavery could never be successfully introduced in that region. Yet when the vote on the bill was finally taken only two southern senators and nine representatives voted against it. Why did so many southern congressmen support it? Most insisted they were supporting the principle of equality among the states, that is, between the free and slave states. Moreover, President Pierce, encouraged by Secretary of War Jefferson Davis and others, threw the full support of the administration behind the measure, and southern Democrats hewed to the party line. Probably the most important reason for southern support of Douglas and his bill lay in the South's reaction to the angry explosion among antislavery northerners.

Southern newspapers, like southern congressmen, initially

gave the Kansas-Nebraska bill a mixed and unexcited treatment. The influential *Richmond Enquirer* thought the South had experienced too much political excitement in 1849–1850 and that four years later there prevailed "a repugnance to agitation." As for the repeal of the Missouri Compromise's ban on slavery, a South Carolina newspaper laconically declared that it would have "to be excused from going into ecstasies over the mere abstract renunciation of gross error." One of the sharpest prophecies came from a North Carolina editor who thought that the Kansas-Nebraska measure would provide "the rallying cry for another antislavery agitation" which would dwarf anything that had preceded it.

The North Carolinian hit the nail on the head: the most important consequence of the Kansas-Nebraska bill for the South, and indeed for the nation, was that northern hostility to it led to the birth in that same year of the Republican party. Dedicated to the central principle of federal prohibition of slavery in the territories, and exclusively northern in its constituency, it was destined soon to outstrip and overshadow the tiny Liberty party of the early 1840s and even the larger Free Soil party of 1848.

Totally unforeseen events in Kansas Territory helped to nurture the newly born Republican party as well as to embarrass Douglas and the Democrats. While Congress was still hotly debating the Kansas-Nebraska bill, antislavery leaders in Massachusetts organized the New England Emigrant Aid Company with the purpose of assisting white adherents of the free-soil doctrine to migrate to Kansas. Grandiose accounts of the plan in such antislavery papers as Greeley's *Tribune* inflamed the fear and anger of Missourians, especially in the western part of the state; in traditional American frontier and rural style they soon formed their own associations of vigilantes or regulators to "save Kansas" from abolitionists and for the South and slavery. Sporadic violence and disputed elections furnished ample grist for sensationalized accounts in partisan newspapers North and South. Ironically, most of the settlers in Kansas were actually more concerned about land titles than anything else, but newspapers and politicians east of the Mississippi saw "Bleeding Kansas" as a crucial struggle between freedom and slavery. Senator Seward himself declared: "Come on, then gentlemen of the slave States. Since there is no escaping your challenge, I accept it in behalf of the cause of freedom. We will engage in competition for the virgin soil of Kansas, and God give the victory to the side which is stronger in numbers as it is in right."

Some proud southerners, all too quick to defend what they saw as the honor of the South, hastened to accept Seward's challenge and began to talk of making Kansas a slave state. Newspapers and public meetings in the South picked up the issue and attempted to inspire a migration of southerners, preferably with slaves, to Kansas. Rhett's *Charleston Mercury*, always in the fire-eating vanguard, trumpeted: "We must send men to Kansas, ready to cast in their lot with the proslavery party there and able to meet Abolitionism on its own issue, and with its own weapons."

Despite all the rhetoric and passion, few southern slaveholders evinced any desire or intention to go to Kansas. Even nearby Arkansans tended to remain in their own state. In Missouri, where the so-called "border ruffians" in the western part of the state acted as champions of southern rights, slavery was already a declining institution, partly because of migration into the state and the rapid rise of the nonslaveholding population.

Despite the realities, "Bleeding Kansas" was a powerful symbol and never more so than in the presidential election year of 1856. Violence in Kansas was climaxed in May 1856 by the so-called "sack of Lawrence" by a band of proslavery men and, in retaliation, the murder of five allegedly proslavery settlers on Pottawatomie Creek by John Brown, four of his sons, and three other antislavery men. In Washington, D.C., at about the same time, Senator Charles Sumner delivered his carefully prepared philippic, "The Crime against Kansas," in which he poured forth shocking personal abuse directed at Stephen A. Douglas, Senator Andrew Butler of South Carolina, and various others who had supported the Kansas-Nebraska Act. Representative Preston Brooks of South Carolina, enraged by the attack on his kinsman Butler, two days later marched into the Senate chamber when that body was not in session, found Sumner at his desk, and proceeded to beat him upon the head with a gutta-percha cane until the bloodied senator collapsed to the floor. Representative Brooks's display of southern chivalry in action was applauded by many— by no means all—southerners, but in the eyes of many northern- ers, Brooks had made a martyr to freedom of Sumner, who suf- fered such severe psychosomatic shock that he remained absent from the Senate for two and a half years.

Such violence in Washington and in Kansas provided a back- drop for the presidential election. The political scene was con- fused enough in any case, for the two-year-old Republican party was not the only new and unprecedented political coalition in the nation. The Native American or Know Nothing party sprang up in 1854 alongside the Republicans. There was an unparalleled influx of immigrants into the country in the decade after 1845, and over a third of them were Irish Catholics. Historically that ethnic group had strong ties with the Democratic party. As the national Whig party fell apart, many northern Whigs succumbed to the rising tides of nativism and anti-Catholicism and joined the ranks of the burgeoning Know Nothings.

In the South, where few of the immigrants went and where there were significant numbers of Catholics only in Maryland and Louisiana, there were different reasons behind the growth of the Know Nothings. Many southern Whigs seemingly preferred anything—even death perhaps—to the idea of throwing in with the hated Democrats. Since the Know Nothings hoped to escape the slavery issue by ignoring it and emphasizing their patriotism and loyalty to the Union, the party was attractive to many south- ern Whigs. First in Maryland and Louisiana, then in Kentucky, Tennessee, and Missouri, the Know Nothings grew impressively. They were not as strong in other southern states but generally managed to compete with the Democrats, who increasingly pre- sented themselves as the protectors of southern rights.

The national Democratic party, in fact, remained bisectional, but, as historian David Potter has suggested, after 1854 its sec- tional equilibrium was badly shaken as another unforeseen con- sequence of the Kansas-Nebraska fight. Northern Democrats suf- fered heavy losses in congressional elections in 1854, so much so that they were significantly outnumbered by southern Democrats in Congress, as in the party's councils. From their position of strength in the party and in the Democratic presidential administrations of the 1850s, southern Democrats were too often tempted to overplay their hands and to grasp for immediate, short-term gains that actually hurt their cause in the long run. As the oldest and still largest national party, however, the Democrats went confidently into the presidential election of 1856. Earlier there had been great uncertainty as to whether the Know Nothings would emerge as the national rival of the Democrats, but when the nativist party finally split into two wings over the slavery issue, the North Americans and the South Americans, the Democrats alone maintained their status as a nationally based, bisectional political party.

With both President Pierce and Douglas handicapped in the North by their roles in the Kansas-Nebraska affair and its aftermath, the Democrats turned for their presidential candidate to a veteran politician from Pennsylvania, James Buchanan. As the nation's minister to Great Britain, he had escaped any involvement in the bruising battles about slavery in the territories but was known to have sympathy for the southern viewpoint. The South Americans and what was left of the Whig party named Millard Fillmore as their candidate. In the South the contest was only between Buchanan and Fillmore, since John C. Frémont, the dashing but politically inexperienced candidate of the Republicans and the North Americans, had virtually no support outside the North. Frémont, in fact, was not on the ticket in any southern state except Delaware, Maryland, Virginia, and Kentucky; only in Delaware did he receive as much as 1 percent of the vote.

With the exclusively northern antislavery Republicans clearly emerging by 1856 as the great challenger of the Democrats in the North, various prominent southerners warned during the campaign that a Republican presidential victory would be ample justification for the southern states to secede. Governor Henry Wise of Virginia declared that the election of a "black Republican" as president "would be an open, overt proclamation of public war."

Robert Toombs stated that "the election of Frémont would be the end of the Union, and ought to be." Numerous southern newspapers struck the same note.

The results of the election brought both satisfaction and concern to the majority in the South. The satisfaction derived from the fact that Buchanan and the Democrats won by carrying all of the southern states save Maryland, which went to Fillmore, plus much of what might be called the Lower North—Pennsylvania, New Jersey, Illinois, Indiana, and California. Just as the Upper South long held out against the pull of southern sectionalism, so the Lower North resisted the lure of the northern sectionalism represented by the Republicans. The Democratic party's national or bisectional basis, badly strained though it was, still proved sufficient to give it victory in 1856.

Southern concern about the election's results arose from the remarkable strength displayed by the Republicans in the North. Frémont carried eleven free states, and the addition of Pennsylvania plus either Indiana or Illinois would have given a two-year-old, exclusively northern party the presidency. The situation was new in American history and inspired fear and anger among many southerners.

Although the majority of southern voters had become Democrats, the opposition of a substantial number of southerners to that party remained strong, and there was far from being a "solid South" in a political sense. Fillmore on the Whig-South American ticket received more than 40 percent of the vote in ten southern states. The South thus remained very much a two-party region even though one of the parties was severely handicapped by its inability to find a northern partner.

Yet the southern majority applauded Buchanan's victory, as they did also a decision of the United States Supreme Court that was rendered in 1857, shortly after Buchanan's inauguration. In the most important part of the Dred Scott decision, the majority of the Supreme Court held that Congress had no power under the Constitution to prohibit slavery in any territory and that, accordingly, that portion of the Missouri Compromise of 1820 had been unconstitutional even before it was repealed in 1854. In addition

Chief Justice Roger B. Taney and two other justices held, in a historically unsound argument, that a Negro could not be a citizen of the United States. While many northern abolitionists objected to the latter assertion, the great storm of anger and suspicion with which Republicans greeted the Dred Scott decision focused on the matter of the territories, since the demand for federal prohibition of slavery there continued to be the glue that held together the powerful but heterogeneous northern coalition. The partisan and untrue charge that the Dred Scott decision was but one more step in a great "Slave Power" conspiracy to extend slavery was one that Seward, Greeley, Abraham Lincoln, and countless other Republicans repeated endlessly. Despite the angry accusations of the Republicans, the South's victory in the Dred Scott decision was a hollow one, and, as events would reveal, extremists in the South were encouraged by it to push their demands farther than the language of the decision actually warranted.

Winning hollow victories, however, became something of a habit for the South, or, to be more exact, for southern Democrats. The next one came in Kansas. There by 1857 were to be found only two hundred or so slaves and apparently a majority of settlers who wished to see neither slavery nor Negroes in the territory. Yet through a complicated series of events the proslavery Kansans proposed a state constitution, known as the Lecompton constitution, which would guarantee to slaveholders already there their permanent property rights in their slaves and would give Kansans the option of voting in a referendum, not on the constitution as a whole, but on whether new slaves could be brought into Kansas. Thus the only choice for Kansas voters was between a constitution that was extremely proslavery and one that was only moderately so.

President Buchanan had originally hoped to give popular sovereignty a fair trial in Kansas and end the prolonged agitation about the matter. Yet with the strong approbation of the southern Democrats who were his long-time friends in Congress and in his cabinet, he decided to throw the full weight of his administration behind the Lecompton constitution and try to persuade Con-

gress to admit Kansas as a state under it. Southern Democrats
thus won another hollow victory, one with grave consequences.

One of the most important intraparty battles in American
history broke out in late 1857. Senator Stephen A. Douglas announced that the Lecompton constitution was not at all what he
meant by popular sovereignty and that he would fight it tooth and
nail. Allied with Republicans who had pilloried him mercilessly
since 1854, Douglas used all of his abundant oratorical and political skills. In doing so his stock among many northern Democrats rose, just as it fell with the southern Democrats. The bitter
struggle in Congress held the nation's excited attention for the
better part of 1858, but by August of that year Buchanan and the
proslavery forces had clearly lost: Kansans, in response to a measure that Congress finally passed, turned down the Lecompton
constitution 11,300 to 1,788. Statehood for Kansas would not
come until 1861, and then, as Douglas had intended from the
first, the North gained another free state.

In 1858, however, Stephen A. Douglas faced more immediate and dangerous problems than those posed for him by the enmity of the southern Democrats. He was running for reelection
to the Senate and faced a quite real prospect of defeat, since the
Buchanan administration was just as determined to beat Douglas
as were the Republicans and their candidate for the Senate, Abraham Lincoln. Because of Douglas's preeminence among northern
Democrats and the double obstacles to his reelection, the South as
well as the rest of the nation watched the Illinois senatorial contest
closely.

As far as the South was concerned, two most important facts
emerged clearly from the debates between Douglas and Lincoln
that preceded the former's victory in holding his senatorship. The
first fact concerned Douglas. During the Lecompton fight Douglas had repeatedly explained how, in his view, popular sovereignty
could result in the exclusion of slavery from a territory. In the
debate at Freeport, Illinois, Douglas said nothing that he had not
said before, but perhaps the nation listened more carefully—and
southerners were infuriated by what they heard. Lincoln and the
Republicans wished to make the Dred Scott decision appear to

have said more than it actually said, for the opinion of Chief Justice Taney that a territorial government could not exclude slavery was not the explicit finding of the majority of the Court. Yet Lincoln, believing that federal prohibition of slavery in the territories was the only reliable and moral policy, put this question to Douglas: "Can the people of a United States Territory, in any lawful way, against the wish of any citizen of the United States, exclude slavery from its limits prior to the formation of a State Constitution?" As Douglas had often maintained earlier, he again asserted his common-sensical belief that slavery, in the last analysis, depended on local legislation and particularly local police regulations for its very survival. If, therefore, the people of a territory were hostile to slavery, they did not have to declare or proclaim against it but merely to refuse to enact the local laws without which slavery could not survive. If Douglas's "Freeport doctrine" made good sense to northern Democrats, it was anathema to a great many southern members of the party, who increasingly hated and feared Douglas as much as any Republican.

The second fact emerging from the Illinois debates that was important to the South had to do with Lincoln. He, like the great majority of Republicans, carefully kept clear of abolitionism and, because of its scorn for the Constitution and unpopularity in the North, he went to great lengths to disavow any sympathy with what might be called the extreme left wing of the antislavery movement. This Lincolnian moderation would have much to do with his later gaining the Republican nomination for the presidency. Yet what was quite clear in 1858 about Lincoln's adherence to the central principle and platform of the Republican party— federal prohibition of slavery in the territories—was that he saw it as having a two-fold function: it would acknowledge the moral wrongness of slavery, which Lincoln stressed and Douglas saw as an abstraction and a gratuitous insult to the South; and the adoption of the principle by the federal government would mean, in Lincoln's words, that "the public mind shall rest in the belief that [slavery] is in the course of ultimate extinction."

Lincoln was thus not an abolitionist but an ultimate extinctionist. The matter was not one that he spoke of frequently nor did he furnish much detail as to just how or when slavery might be ended or what was to happen to the emancipated blacks. He indicated that "ultimate" might mean a hundred years and that what he "would most desire would be the separation of the white and black races," that is, the colonization of the blacks outside of the United States. Though not as extreme in his avowals of white supremacy and black inferiority as Douglas, Lincoln on several occasions stressed his belief that there was a physical difference between whites and blacks which would "forever forbid the two races living together on terms of social and political equality." He concluded, "I as much as any other man am in favor of having the superior position assigned to the white race."

Ambiguous though Lincoln's position and views about emancipation and race relations may have been, they reflected the ambiguities in the Republican party as a whole. Moreover, the matter tended to be moot in Illinois, as in much of the North, where there were no slaves and very few blacks. In the South, of course, the situation was quite different, and ambiguities about the future of the blacks were not to be tolerated. The distinction between abolition and ultimate extinction, therefore, seemed picayune or even nonexistent in many southern eyes. If the Illinois debates in 1858 confirmed the South's growing hostility to Douglas, they also reinforced the South's oversimplified stereotype of all Republicans, including the newly prominent Lincoln, as thinly disguised abolitionists.

That southern perception of Republicans gained immense new power and emotional depth after October 1859. John Brown in that month led his small band of abolitionist followers in the abortive attempt to spark off a wave of slave insurrections in the South by seizing the federal arsenal at Harpers Ferry, Virginia. No slaves in the area responded, and Brown and his group were quickly overcome, with Brown subsequently tried, convicted, and hanged. The slave insurrections that Brown had hoped to start were the ultimate horror and societal nightmare of white southerners. More than that, however, the South was deeply angered and aggrieved by the reaction of many northerners to the raid and to Brown himself.

Despite the repeated efforts of leading Republicans such as Seward and Lincoln to disavow any responsibility for or approval of Brown's action, a large number of northerners clearly viewed him as a heroic martyr in the cause of freedom. On the day of his death huge memorial services were held in various northern cities, church bells tolled, and New England's leading intellectuals, such as Ralph Waldo Emerson and Henry David Thoreau, joined the abolitionists in extravagant praise of one whom Thoreau compared to Jesus Christ and called "an angel of light."

Seward had earlier spoken of an "irrepressible conflict" between slavery and freedom, but, southerners asserted, Brown had actually started it. The Tennessee legislature passed resolutions declaring the affair at Harpers Ferry to be "the natural fruit" of the treasonable doctrine advanced by Seward as the foremost leader of the "Black Republicans," and a Mississippi political leader advised his constituents that "Mr. Seward and his followers . . . have declared war on us." A prominent South Carolinian put the matter this way: "Every village bell which tolled its solemn note at the execution of Brown proclaims to the South the approbation [by] that village of insurrection and servile war." John Brown's actual mission, Jefferson Davis noted, was "to incite slaves to murder helpless women and children."

Not only individuals but leading southern newspapers indicated the extent and gravity of the South's reaction. The *Baltimore Sun* declared that the South could no longer afford to "live under a government, the majority of whose subjects or citizens regard John Brown as a martyr and a Christian hero, rather than a murderer and robber." The *Richmond Examiner* asserted that the John Brown affair had "advanced the cause of disunion more than any other event that has happened" since the formation of the nation. Clearly the South, in the aftermath of Harpers Ferry, approached the presidential election of 1860 in a highly excited, disturbed frame of mind.

As had happened so often since 1846, rising sectional passions in the nation at large were sharply reflected and dramatized in Congress. From December 5, 1859 (three days after John Brown was hanged) until February 1, 1860, the House of Representatives remained locked in an intense, paralyzing battle over the election of a Speaker. The Democrats controlled the Senate, but Republicans outnumbered them in the House, 109 to 101, with Whig-Americans holding 27 seats.

Republican efforts to name John Sherman of Ohio as Speaker were bitterly opposed by southern congressmen on the ground that Sherman had earlier endorsed a Republican plan to prepare and distribute 100,000 copies of an abridgment of Hinton R. Helper's *The Impending Crisis*. A nonslaveholding white from North Carolina, Helper had written an angry polemic charging that slavery had impeded and hurt the South economically and that the nonslaveholding whites were harmed most of all by the peculiar institution. Blatantly anti-Negro as well as antislavery, Helper challenged one of the central pillars of southern proslavery thought by appealing to the nonslaveholders and by denying that the racial division between blacks and whites had obliterated class divisions among whites.

Southerners denounced Helper as an incendiary traitor, banned his book, and writhed furiously about the Republicans' plan to use the abridged version in the 1860 campaign. The Republicans in the House were finally forced to drop Sherman and succeeded in having another Republican elected as Speaker, but some of the southern members had shown during the prolonged battle that they no longer cared how long the House remained unorganized and the federal government paralyzed.

Many southerners believed that disunion sentiment had increased in the section, but the fire-eaters remained a distinct minority in actually wanting disunion and doing everything possible to help bring it about. Proslavery extremists in the South, more concerned about their state and local power than about the national basis of the Democratic party, increasingly embraced abstractions and radical demands. One such demand that appeared prominently in the 1850s was that the African slave trade, stopped by federal law after 1808, should be reopened. Though pushed for a while by Rhett's *Charleston Mercury* and other fire-eating newspapers and politicians, the idea was divisive and never gained widespread support. Most southerners proved quite capable of holding a benign image of slavery itself while rejecting the African slave trade as barbarous and cruel. By the end of the decade, even advocates of the trade's reopening had to admit that the southern majority was against it.

In Congress the southern Democrats hit on a device, indeed an abstraction, that would demonstrate their own unlimited devotion to slavery and to the South and at the same time, they hoped, prove a stumbling block to Douglas and his northern Democratic allies. In the sectional crisis of 1849–1850, Calhoun had advanced to the extreme position that Congress had an obligation under the Constitution to provide federal protection for slavery in a territory. Most southerners then had been unwilling to go to such a seemingly unrealistic, far-fetched position, and had rejected it. By 1859-1860, however, Douglas had amply demonstrated how he meant for popular sovereignty to exclude slavery from the territories, and Chief Justice Taney, though not the majority of the Supreme Court, had indicated his belief that neither Congress nor a territorial legislature authorized by Congress could exclude slavery from a territory.

The southern Democrats responded to all these developments by embracing the extreme Calhounian argument and demanding a congressional slave code for the territories, something Douglas and his allies utterly rejected. Jefferson Davis introduced resolutions embodying much of the southern position in the Senate in February 1860 and, over the strong but futile protests of the northern Democratic minority, succeeded in having the Democratic caucus of the Senate adopt a version of Davis's resolutions. The Democratic national convention was less than three months away, and the idea was fast catching on among some southern politicians that if that convention refused to endorse a congressional slave code, then the southern delegates should withdraw from the convention. Different persons had various motives in advocating such a course of action, and many clearly thought they could force the northern Democrats to make concessions to the South and to accept a compromise candidate. But fire-eaters such as Rhett and Yancey saw the disruption of the national Democratic party as the essential prelude to their ultimate goal of secession and the creation of a separate southern nation.

In the Democratic national convention that met in Charleston, South Carolina, in April 1860, the northern Democrats were fully represented even though their numbers in Congress had fallen drastically since 1854. Most of them recognized Stephen A. Douglas as the only candidate who might defeat the Republicans in the North, and a majority of the delegates at the convention supported Douglas. Many of the southern Democrats, however, were determined to stop at nothing to prevent Douglas's nomination. Their chances of doing so were good, too, for since the 1830s the party had operated under a rule that required a candidate to have a two-thirds majority to win the nomination.

For ten hectic, tense days the Democrats battled in Charleston. The platform committee finally presented a majority report calling for a congressional slave code in the territories, and a minority report, supported mostly by northern Democrats, that would leave to the Supreme Court the further clarification of the powers over slavery in the territories possessed by Congress and territorial legislatures. When the convention voted, 165 to 138, in favor of adopting the minority report, the delegates from Alabama led in the withdrawal from the convention. The delegates from South Carolina, Georgia, Florida, Mississippi, Louisiana, and Texas soon followed, as well as most of those from Arkansas and a third of those from Delaware. In 1848 Yancey of Alabama and only one follower had bolted the Democratic convention on the issue of slavery in the territories, but in 1860 all of the delegates from the Deep South walked out. When the chair ruled that a two-thirds majority of the original number of delegate votes was still required to nominate the presidential candidate, and the Douglas forces could never quite gain that many, the convention finally voted to adjourn and meet again in Baltimore in June.

At the Baltimore convention the sectional split in the last remaining national political party became complete. There were contested delegations from several of the states of the Deep South; when the convention voted in favor of the delegations that favored

Douglas, Democrats from the Upper South, led off by Virginia, now did what those from the Deep South had done at Charleston: bolted the party. Douglas, with Herschel V. Johnson of Georgia as his running mate, thus became the nominee of what was left of the regular Democratic party. The bolters from the southern states plus a handful of Buchanan supporters from the North met in a separate hall in Baltimore and nominated John C. Breckinridge of Kentucky as their presidential candidate, one who endorsed the call for a congressional slave code but rejected disunionism.

Not all southerners, by any means, were oblivious to the dangers that appeared to loom ahead. The *Memphis Appeal*, for example, issued a warning: "It has been the just pride of the Democratic party that it was *National* . . . indeed it is believed that there is not a precinct in the whole Union in which Democratic votes are not polled." On the other hand, the "odium of the Black-Republican party has been that it is *Sectional* without organization of members in one-half of the States of the Union." Were southerners now to allow a group of "restless and reckless or misguided men" to destroy the national party and build up a southern party as sectional as the Republicans? The *Appeal* urged loyal Democrats not to follow those fire-eating Democrats such as Yancey whose aim was to "precipitate the Cotton States into a Revolution."

Former Whigs in the South also reacted strongly against the increasing danger to the Union. Some of them, such as Alexander Stephens of Georgia, supported Douglas. Others, however, especially in the Upper South, looked to the establishment of a Constitutional Union party with its own presidential ticket as the wisest course. The old Whigs, often known simply as the Opposition party, showed impressive strength in state and local elections throughout the Upper South in the late 1850s. Various leaders, such as John J. Crittenden of Kentucky and Alexander H. Stuart of Virginia, kept in touch with former Whig allies in the North in the hope of rebuilding a national coalition that could somehow play down or ignore the slavery question and emphasize the Union. In May 1860, in Baltimore, these Constitutional Unionists named John Bell of Tennessee as their presidential candidate and Edward Everett of Massachusetts for the vice presidency.

The Republicans at Chicago named Abraham Lincoln as their candidate and broadened their appeal in the North by adding a group of economic demands to their central principle of excluding slavery from the territories. Horace Greeley of the *New York Tribune* aptly explained the Republican strategy in a private letter: "I want to succeed this time, yet I know the country [the North] is not Anti-Slavery. It will only swallow a little Anti-Slavery in a great deal of sweetening. An Anti-Slavery man *per se* cannot be elected; but a Tariff, River-and-Harbor, Pacific Railroad, Free-Homestead man *may* succeed *although* he is Anti-Slavery." In short, Greeley and most other Republican leaders well knew that to win the presidency in 1860 they had only to hold the eleven northern states they had carried in 1856 and add Pennsylvania plus Indiana or Illinois or New Jersey. The split in the Democratic party could not but make the task easier for the Republicans.

The campaign in 1860 was one of the strangest in American history. Not only were there four major candidates—Bell, Breckinridge, Douglas, and Lincoln—but, in a sense, there were two separate campaigns: one between Lincoln and Douglas in the North and one between Breckinridge and Bell in the South. The sectional nature of Breckinridge's candidacy is indicated by the fact that he did not get as much as 6 percent of the vote in any northern or free state except Oregon, California, and Connecticut (all three of which Lincoln won). Lincoln, on the other hand, was not even on the ballot in ten southern states, and while he received 23 percent of the vote in Delaware, which was only nominally a slave state, and 10 percent in Missouri, he got only a tiny number of votes in Virginia and Kentucky.

Another strange feature of the campaign was that one of the issues, the possible secession of some of the southern states in case the Republicans won, remained half hidden and deliberately ignored by the two sectional parties. The Breckinridge Democrats emphasized their support for a congressional slave code in the territories—the magic symbol of southern rights—but also stressed their alleged Unionism and played down the possibility of secession. Likewise, the Republicans scoffed at the idea of southern disunionism and, as they had done all along, dismissed the southern threats of it as mere bluff and bluster designed to scare the North into yielding to the South's demands. Lincoln made no public statements at all during the campaign but privately expressed a belief similar to what he had said publicly in 1856: all the southern talk about secession was "humbug, nothing but folly."

Douglas totally disagreed with Lincoln's reasoning and, alone among major figures in American political life at the time, tried to carry the message into all sections of the country that the Union was imperiled. Defying the strong tradition that prohibited a presidential candidate from openly campaigning and speaking, Douglas tried to warn northern audiences that the Union was in danger and to advise southern ones that there was no such thing as a constitutional right to secede, that secession was a synonym for treason and a sure pathway to disaster. "It was, of course, in Douglas's interest to emphasize these realities," the historian David Potter has written, "but in his manner of doing it, he exceeded himself and showed a sense of public responsibility unmatched by any of the other candidates."

The labors of Douglas were in vain, for Lincoln, receiving only 39 percent of the total popular vote, nevertheless won the presidency by gaining the electoral votes of all of the northern states save three of New Jersey's. Moreover, Lincoln won a majority of the popular vote in all of the states he carried except Oregon, California, and New Jersey, none of which he had to have to win. While Douglas came in second in the popular vote, he won the electoral votes of only Missouri plus three of New Jersey's.

In the South, Bell carried Virginia, Kentucky, and Tennessee. Breckinridge won in eleven states, but won statewide majorities in only four states. In the South as a whole the opponents of Breckinridge won a combined total of 55 percent of the popular vote and had a majority of the vote in ten states. Clearly there was no popular mandate for southern extremism and certainly not for disunionism, which Breckinridge disavowed, though most southern extremists were among his supporters.

Unionism in the South, as reflected in the 1860 voting, was still concentrated in the region's few large cities and in the areas of greatest slaveholding, that is, in the places where the southern Whigs had traditionally been strongest. One close study of a large number of southern counties revealed that those with the lowest proportion of slaves in their population cast the largest percent of votes for Breckinridge and the party whose chief claim was, above all else, to protect slavery and southern rights. With the bulk of the large slaveholders voting one way and the nonslaveholders plus small holders voting another, one can but wonder about the so-called hegemony which some historians allege the large slaveholders to have enjoyed in the antebellum South. As for zeal in defending slavery, nonslaveholders apparently were in the front ranks, and that was probably because they could not possibly imagine any other racial arrangement which they as white southerners would tolerate. Too, in voting for Breckinridge they were voting Democratic, as most of them had long been wont to do.

Strangely enough, despite all of the southern threats about secession if the Republicans should win the presidency—and they had not won control of Congress—the limited transfer of power that Lincoln's triumph signaled came as a shock to most southerners. Largely a rural and provincial people, they had been isolated from the Republicans since that party's birth, and, just as so many Republicans held their stereotyped views of the South and its people, southerners clung to their melodramatic distortions and oversimplifications about the "Black Republicans" and the "reincarnated John Brown" whom northern voters had elected to the presidency. Lincoln and his party had ridiculed the idea of secession and dismissed the threat as meaningless. The winter of 1860–1861 would test the accuracy of that view and bring a critical time of great uncertainty and confusion to the South as a whole as well as to the rest of the nation.

CHAPTER FOUR

Secession and War
1860–1865

SOUTHERNERS BY 1860 had achieved remarkable unity in defense of slavery and were profoundly fearful of what a Republican administration might do, no matter how gradually or subtly, to weaken or perhaps ultimately to destroy what they regarded as both the cornerstone of southern civilization and the guarantor of white liberty and equality. Many politically conscious southerners, indeed, probably a majority, had also come to venerate what they considered to be two basic constitutional principles: first, that a sovereign state possessed the right to secede from the Union and second, that the federal government could not lawfully use force or coercion against a sovereign state. Beyond these fundamental and rather abstract notions, however, there were deep divisions among southerners as to the wisdom, timing, and method of actually effecting secession, and the crucial winter of 1860–1861 would reveal these deep fissures among the voters of the slaveholding states.

South Carolina had early attained a degree of political unity and a commitment to radical action that was not true of other southern states, and it was no accident that following Lincoln's election South Carolina led the parade for secession. Late in 1859, after the Harpers Ferry affair threw South Carolinians into what one historian has aptly described as a profound and prolonged "crisis of fear," South Carolina attempted to cooperate with Virginia and other southern states in considering their situation and planning joint action. That attempt failed, as did subsequent efforts aimed at cooperative action in the following year.

A dangerously proud people, South Carolinians were quite aware that the Republicans had sneeringly dismissed or ridiculed southern threats of secession if Lincoln should win the presidency. "It would appear certain," the British consul at Charleston commented, "that South Carolina must either secede at all hazards, on or before the inauguration of Mr. Lincoln, or be content to have herself exhibited to the ridicule of the world." Determined not to be laughed at, and assured by leaders in the Deep South that those states would quickly take similar action, the South Carolina legislature voted on November 10, 1860—four days after Lincoln's victory—to hold an election on December 6 for a convention that would meet on December 20. The secessionists emphasized their intention to pursue a peaceful policy and minimized the danger of war. (Ironically, some Republicans initially took a similar stand in the early phase of the secession crisis, for they feared that otherwise northern public opinion might demand a compromise.) On December 20, the South Carolina convention voted unanimously to secede.

South Carolina's bold action marked the beginning of a swift chain of events in the Deep South. By February 1, 1861, six other states—Georgia, Florida, Alabama, Mississippi, Louisiana, and Texas—elected conventions which in turn voted for immediate secession. Unlike South Carolina's deceptive unanimity, however, the other states were far from unanimous, and the elections for the conventions were hard fought. The question of how much popular support there was for secession even in the Deep South was controversial at the time, for Lincoln and the Republicans long clung to and were much influenced by their belief that most southerners were Unionists at heart. Moreover, historians still do not agree about the matter.

The problem of determining the amount of popular support for secession in the Deep South is compounded by the fact that there were no party labels in the elections. Since virtually all voters agreed on the necessity of defending southern rights (meaning, in effect, slavery) and regarded the Republican triumph as a threat to or even a denial of the liberty and equality of southern whites, the disagreement tended to be between the immediate secessionists and the cooperationists. The latter group, obviously wanting to slow things down, argued that the safer, surer way to protect southern rights was for the slaveholding states to confer and act in concert, that such unity might lead the Republicans to make meaningful concessions to the South, and that if none were forthcoming, then a unified approach to secession would be more likely to succeed. Although some cooperationists were merely prudent secessionists, some were half-camouflaged or intimidated Unionists. A newspaper in New Orleans put the matter succinctly: "Here . . . nobody knows exactly what cooperation means. With some it means delay, with some conference with other states, with some it means submission [to a Republican president]."

Regardless of the ambiguity involved in cooperationism, candidates of that persuasion polled a significant minority of votes in Mississippi, Florida, and Alabama in December 1860. In Georgia's election of convention delegates in January 1861, the secessionists won by such a small margin—the most generous estimate is 44,152 to 41,632—that some historians argue that the cooperationists actually polled a narrow majority of the votes. The balloting in Louisiana was similarly close. Despite the strong showing of the cooperationists, especially in Georgia and Louisiana, the immediate secessionists controlled all of the conventions in the cotton states. And since an indeterminable number of the cooperationists were, after all, prudent or go-slow secessionists, historian Charles Roland seems correct in the assertion that, "Notwithstanding the presence of large Unionist minorities in some of the [Deep South] states, it is doubtful that any similar political rupture in modern history has been supported by as high a proportion of the population."

The greatest worry of the secessionists, however, had to do with the opposition of majorities in the Upper South to immediate secession. The seven Deep South states which had seceded by February 1, 1861, sent delegates to Montgomery, Alabama, on February 4, who drew up a provisional constitution for the Confederate States of America and elected Jefferson Davis, a former Democrat of Mississippi, as provisional president, and Alexander Stephens, a former Whig of Georgia, as provisional vice president. The proud new Confederacy was, nevertheless, an obviously and embarrassingly half-built house as long as it was without all or a substantial part of the remaining eight slave states, including perhaps the one most conspicuously missing, the cradle of southern institutions and customs, Virginia.

Resentment against South Carolina's allegedly hasty action in seceding ran strong in various parts of the Upper South. A newspaper in Charlottesville, Virginia, for example, declared that it "hated South Carolina for precipitating secession," and one in Wilmington, North Carolina, asserted that "There are no two adjoining states in the Union whose people have so little community of feeling as North and South Carolina."

The Tar Heel editor exaggerated, but perhaps the most fundamental fact was that the white people of the Upper South were not as obsessively preoccupied with slavery as were those of the Deep South. In the seven states that initially seceded, Texas alone had a black population of less than 40 percent, and it was still very much a developing, frontier state. But in Virginia, North Carolina, Tennessee, Arkansas, and Missouri—five states that held their elections in February 1861—the black population averaged less than 30 percent. Not only did most of the Upper South states have strong economic ties with the North, but their Unionism was also much stronger than that of the Deep South. First in Virginia and then in the other four states the voters indicated by strong majorities their opposition to immediate secession. Their continuing Unionism was highly qualified, however, and certainly involved no sanction for the federal government's use of coercion against a sovereign state.

A key factor in dampening the secessionist impulse in the Upper South was the lingering hope of compromise and of concessions to the South. Among the most prominent and active supporters of compromise and intersectional peace were Senators Stephen A. Douglas of Illinois and John J. Crittenden of Kentucky. While President Buchanan called in vain for a constitutional convention to deal with the crisis, the Senate named a distinguished Committee of Thirteen which included such prominent leaders as Douglas, Crittenden, Seward, Davis, and Toombs. The last two, spokesmen for southern Democrats, conditioned their acceptance of any compromise measure upon the Republican assent also, since that party would control the presidency.

Senator Crittenden, following in the footsteps of Clay, presented a package of proposed amendments to the Constitution, the most important of which called for extending the old line of 36°30' in the nation's territory "now held, or hereafter acquired," prohibiting slavery north of that line, and not only allowing it south of the line but granting it federal protection during the territorial stage. Whether the South would actually gain a future slave state or states from the New Mexico Territory, even with the concession concerning federal protection, was debatable at the time and has remained controversial. What was indisputable, however, was that the proposal flew directly against the central principle of the Republican party, and with the private encouragement of President-elect Lincoln, the Republicans repeatedly killed all chances of its passage.

Just as Crittenden's efforts to forge a compromise failed, so too did Virginia's moves to find a way out of the critical impasse. In response to the Old Dominion's call, delegates from the Upper South and from most of the northern states assembled in Washington in February 1861 for a Peace Conference. With northern Democrats and Whig-Americans from the Upper South lending the strongest support, the conference ended by calling for a multipart constitutional amendment much like Crittenden's proposal, but it too got nowhere in Congress. Although warning voices were raised in all parts of the country, no one knew for certain that with the death of the compromise efforts, the nation was headed straight for what the great majority of people in all sections least wanted and most feared: a bloody civil war, the costliest in terms of American lives in history.

By the time Lincoln took office in early March 1861, federal properties in the Deep South, with two important exceptions, had been taken over by state authorities. The exceptions were Fort Sumter in Charleston harbor and Fort Pickens at Pensacola, Florida. The former, for historic as well as strategic and political reasons, loomed largest as a symbol—to northerners as a symbol of the federal government's lawful authority in an indissoluble Union and to southerners as a symbol of an incongruous, humiliating, and unacceptable foreign garrison on ground that had become part of a new and proudly independent nation.

Lincoln learned the day after his inauguration that the federal garrison at Fort Sumter had provisions that would last for only four to six weeks. Most members of Lincoln's cabinet as well as his top military advisor believed that there was no acceptable alternative to the evacuation of the garrison, and Secretary of State Seward, acting on his own initiative and without the knowledge of Lincoln, indirectly conveyed assurances to Confederate representatives in Washington that Sumter would soon be evacuated. Lincoln, however, ultimately arrived at the decision only to send provisions to the federal garrison at Sumter and to have South Carolina authorities informed well in advance that he was doing so and would make no effort to send in reinforcements if the reprovisioning was permitted to take place peacefully. Lincoln thus opted for the maintenance of the status quo in Charleston harbor.

Confederate President Davis and his cabinet, finding the status quo in Charleston no longer tolerable and believing themselves to have been deliberately lied to by Seward, opted for war. On orders from the Confederate government, General Pierre G.T. Beauregard opened fire on the federal garrison at Fort Sumter on April 12, 1861, and the Civil War had begun. If it began in a manner that unified much of the North behind Lincoln, it also helped the Confederates substantially to complete their half-built nation. Lincoln called upon all the states to supply a total of 75,000 volunteer troops to suppress what he viewed as insurrectionary "combinations" in the Deep South. Confronted thereby with an inescapable choice of assisting the federal cause or seceding, four states of the Upper South—Virginia, North Carolina, Tennessee, and Arkansas—hastened to join the Confederacy. Although Maryland, Kentucky, and Missouri contained numerous Confederate sympathizers, all three states remained in the Union.

Although leaders on both sides naively expected a short and easy struggle, the war actually lasted four years, and during that time politics North and South necessarily became secondary to and greatly influenced by military developments. In the South, at least in theory, partisan labels were dropped and partisan politics supposedly buried for the duration of the struggle. In reality the situation was quite different, and politics, much of it petty and self-defeating, went on throughout the war.

In the months following the Confederacy's victory at First Bull Run, or Manassas, in July 1861, the South suffered a series of military setbacks. First Fort Hatteras and then Roanoke Island off the North Carolina coast fell to the federals; West Virginia separated itself from Virginia and thus from the Confederacy, and Confederate military efforts to hold the area failed; a Confederate army in Kentucky met defeat; and, perhaps most important, Forts Henry and Donelson on the Tennessee and Cumberland Rivers were captured by federal armies. In Virginia by the spring of 1862, Federal General George B. McClellan commanded a huge army that aimed at capturing Richmond, the Confederate capital.

Seeking a scapegoat for all of the troubles, many Confederates, including some who were highly placed, began to blame Jefferson Davis. James H. Hammond of South Carolina, for example, advised a friend in the Confederate Congress, "Impeach Jeff Davis for incompetency and call a convention of the States." A distinguished Georgian in Richmond informed his wife that Congress would depose Davis if it "had any more confidence in [Vice President] Stephens than in him." Stephens, in fact, largely abandoned his post in Richmond, returned to his plantation in Georgia, and gradually emerged as one of the severest critics of Davis and his policies. In the Senate, Louis T. Wigfall of Texas became a conspicuously bitter foe of the Confederate president, and there were several like him in the House. Speaking through the columns of the *Charleston Mercury*, Robert Barnwell Rhett became an early and vehement foe of the Davis administration and its policies. The essentially defensive strategy that the Richmond government pursued became a particular object of Rhett's wrath, and *Mercury* editorials were soon warning of alleged executive usurpation of power and the threat of military despotism.

Southerners argued at the time that the absence of formal, organized political parties within the Confederacy made for greater unity and allowed them to concentrate on trying to win the war and establish their independence. Some historians have suggested, however, that the absence of organized political parties may actually have been a source of weakness for the Confederacy. Not only did Davis have no organized party behind him and the policies of his administration, but there was no loyal opposition with a responsibility to formulate alternatives and offer constructive criticism. As a result, attacks on Davis and the administration remained highly personal and often petty. Above all, as the Confederate government moved in 1862 to adopt more drastic measures in pursuit of victory and national independence, the opponents and critics turned to the familiar cry of states' rights and used that weapon against the Richmond government. Those who did so obviously forgot or did not care that the principle of states' rights had always been not an end in itself but a means to an end, a weapon that southerners after about 1820 had found useful in trying to defend a variety of their sectional interests, including, above all, slavery. Perhaps some southerners had simply become so accustomed to the nay-saying role of a fearful yet proud, defiant minority that a different approach in the different circumstances of an all-out war for southern independence became an impossibility for them.

Neither Jefferson Davis nor numerous other Confederates let old-time scruples about states' rights hamstring them. Elected unanimously and without opposition to a full term as president of the Confederacy in November 1861, Davis took the lead in calling for a series of bold, nationalistic measures. The first of these was conscription, the first such act in American history. Asking Congress in March 1862 for power to draft into the army for the duration of the war all eligible men between the ages of eighteen and thirty-five, Davis gained support for the unprecedented policy from a wide range of prominent people, including General

Robert E. Lee and even Rhett. Congress passed the act in April 1862 by a vote of more than two to one, but conscription became the focus for the most serious, long-lasting political conflict within the Confederacy, that between the nationalists led by Davis and the various champions of states' rights.

None were louder and more persistent in their states' rights battles against the Confederate government than Governor Joseph E. Brown of Georgia. A shrewd, stubborn politician who claimed to represent the yeoman farmers and mountain folk, Brown informed Davis that the conscription act was a "bold and dangerous usurpation by Congress of the reserved rights of the states" and that it was "subversive of [Georgia's] sovereignty and at war with all the principles for the support of which Georgia entered this revolution." Alexander Stephens, Robert Toombs, and others joined in the chorus of opposition.

Even more serious in the long run than the objections to conscription from prominent southerners was the conflict of social classes that the measure inspired. Allegedly refining and reforming the system, Congress in the fall of 1862 provided that owners or overseers of twenty or more slaves were exempted from the draft. Since the great majority of the Confederate army came from the ranks of the nonslaveholders, the "twenty nigger law," as it was contemptuously called by its critics, inspired widespread grumbling among the rank-and-file. They angrily charged that it was "a rich man's war but a poor man's fight."

Undaunted by the critics and supported by majorities in Congress, Davis pushed ahead with what he regarded as essential measures for southern victory. Even before the passage of the conscription act, Congress had authorized the president to suspend the writ of habeas corpus and to declare martial law in places he judged to be in danger of attack. Although subsequent legislation limited the sweeping power initially given to Davis, the basic challenge to the South's vaunted individualism remained alive throughout the war.

Despite internal dissension, Confederate hopes rose in the summer of 1862 as Lee checked McClellan's army before Richmond, and the ambitious federal campaign there collapsed. Lee's army was itself checked, however, in the bloody battle at Antietam (Sharpsburg) in September 1862, a major turning point in the war for several reasons. The outcome of that battle suggested to the British government that its diplomatic recognition of the Confederacy would be premature and unwise, and Britain never again came as close to recognizing the new southern nation as it did in the late summer of 1862.

Furthermore, in a move that had profound effects on the South as well as on the outcome and nature of the war, Lincoln seized on the federal victory at Antietam to broaden the war aims of the United States. From the outset of the war and through its first year and a half, he had repeatedly insisted that the North's sole purpose in the war was to preserve the Union. The destruction of slavery, he maintained in both words and deeds, was not the purpose of the war. For a variety of military, diplomatic, and political reasons, however, Lincoln significantly modified United States policy in September 1862 when he issued a preliminary proclamation warning slaveholders in those areas "in rebellion" that on January 1, 1863, he would declare their slaves "forever free" and that the United States government and military forces would do no act "to repress such persons . . . in any efforts they make for their actual freedom." When Lincoln issued the final Emancipation Proclamation on the date he had indicated and the United States concurrently began enlisting black soldiers and actively recruiting them in the conquered areas of the South, the war had indeed entered a new phase. Confederates would eventually be forced to think about and then finally to debate their own ultimate purposes in the war.

Confederates high and low initially regarded Lincoln's emancipation policy with cold fury and contempt. President Davis in a message to Congress charged that Lincoln was trying to incite insurrections among the slaves and that the measure was "the crowning proof of the true nature of the designs" of the Republican party and its first president. The Confederate Congress issued an address to the southern people which suggested, among other things, that Lincoln "sought to convert the South into a San

Domingo, by appealing to the cupidity, lusts, ambitions, and ferocity of the slave."

To the subsequent and great satisfaction of the Confederates, no slave insurrections occurred. This was certainly not because the slaves were happy in their bondage, as white southerners constantly kept assuring themselves, but because the blacks had other, less dangerous and less self-destructive ways of expressing their yearning for freedom. For one thing, when they could they fought in the Union army. By the late summer of 1864, Lincoln answered racist taunts of his political enemies in the North in this way: "No human power can subdue this rebellion without using the Emancipation lever as I have done. Freedom has given us the control of 200,000 able bodied [black] men, born and raised on southern soil. It will give us more yet. . . . My enemies condemn my emancipation policy. Let them prove by the history of the war, that we can restore the Union without it."

Just as Lincoln had to contend with bitter opposition in the North, so Davis did in the South. With Confederate morale running low after the great Union victories at Gettysburg and Vicksburg in July 1863, the southern elections in the fall of that year brought a significant reduction in the number of congressmen who supported the Davis administration. The electoral results were ambiguous, for not only were there no party lines, but large parts of Arkansas, Louisiana, Mississippi, and Tennessee—not to mention Kentucky and Missouri, which the Confederacy claimed but never actually controlled—were occupied by the federals. Confederate congressmen from those federally-controlled areas tended to support Davis but they actually represented Confederates in exile. Despite all the ambiguities, one careful estimate is that the number of opponents of the Davis administration rose in the House from 26 to 41 out of 106 districts, and in the Senate from 11 to 12 in a full membership of 26. Davis indeed faced greater political problems after May 1864, when the Confederacy's Second Congress convened, but by and large he and his administration remained in control of the war effort.

Aside from the financial problem, which the Confederate

government constantly grappled with but never solved, perhaps the most urgent matter was manpower for the army. As the Confederacy repeatedly widened the net of its draft by extending the age limits and tightening up on exemptions, it also began to consider the vast source of black manpower which the Union, but not the Confederacy, had begun to tap. Late in 1863 Davis urged Congress to pass a law providing for the impressment of free and slave black males and their use in noncombatant military duties. In February 1864 Congress accordingly authorized the army's use of up to 20,000 blacks as cooks, teamsters, laborers, and such. Although Davis himself admitted subsequently that the law did not work too well, it at least indicated that southerners too were being forced by the exigencies of the war to do what Lincoln and the North had already done: to consider radical, even desperate measures to gain manpower and military advantage.

As early as 1863 a few editors and political leaders in the Deep South began to suggest that the Confederacy should consider the freeing and arming of its slaves. With much of Mississippi overrun by federal troops even before Vicksburg fell, the unthinkable possibility of the ultimate defeat of the Confederacy began to lurk in the minds of some men in that area. The *Jackson Mississippian*, for example, in the late summer of 1863 declared that either the Confederacy must use the Negroes or "the enemy will employ them against us." To "forestall Lincoln," the newspaper urged that the blacks should "be declared free, placed in the ranks, and told to fight for their homes and country." The editor admitted that such a step would "revolutionize" the South's "industrial system" but argued that if Lincoln succeeded in "arming our slaves against us, he will succeed in making them our masters" and would "reverse the social order of things at the South." But if he were "checkmated in time, our liberties will remain intact; the land will be ours, and the industrial system of the country still controlled by Southern men."

Beyond the immediate military advantages of a Confederate policy of emancipation, the *Mississippian* noted two additional arguments in favor of the move. It would bring "speedy recognition" of the Confederacy by the European powers and prove to

Europe that, "although slavery is one of the principles that we started to fight for, yet it falls far short of being the chief one" and that "for the sake of our liberty, we are capable of any personal sacrifice." At home the policy would "prove to our soldiers, three-fourths of whom never owned a negro, that it is not 'the rich man's war and the poor man's fight,' but a war for the most sacred of all principles, for the dearest of all rights—the right to govern ourselves."

The Jackson newspaper was not alone in thinking and expressing highly unorthodox things about slavery. James L. Alcorn, prominent Whig leader in Mississippi, in an address to the legislature of that state attacked the Confederate government's diplomatic record with reference to the slavery question and emphasized that the war was not exclusively to save the peculiar institution but had a higher purpose—the right of self-government. Alcorn urged a Confederate change on slavery to win European recognition. In Alabama, also sorely threatened by federal troops, scattered voices raised the question of how the Confederacy might best counter Lincoln's policy of emancipating and enlisting the blacks. The *Mobile Register*, an influential supporter of the Richmond government, admitted that there were differences of opinion among white southerners about the military use of slaves, with some holding that "it is not safe, in any event, to employ our slaves as soldiers, and that such a proceeding would be incompatible with the maintenance of the institution itself." The answer to that, argued the *Register*, was that "Yankee success is death to the institution, as well as to its masters, and that any peril should be confronted to avoid it." Insisting that Confederates could beat the federals in recruiting blacks as well as make them fight better, the Mobile newspaper concluded that if necessity forced the use of Negro soldiers "to beat the enemy and conquer independence and peace, there is no argument of doubtful expediency to counterbalance the superlative end."

Confederate leaders in Richmond may well have been aware of the political dynamite about which certain Mississippians and Alabamians were beginning to talk. With Robert E. Lee's army intact, however, most Virginians did not feel as perilously threatened as did those in parts of the Deep South. Moreover, the influential Richmond newspapers largely ignored the debate concerning the Confederacy's policy on slavery that had begun in the remote hinterland.

One who did not ignore the nascent controversy and the realities that lay behind it was Patrick R. Cleburne, a major general in the Confederate Army of Tennessee. Fresh from the humiliating Confederate defeat at Chattanooga and in winter quarters in northern Georgia, Cleburne late in 1863 worried about the large Federal army that General William T. Sherman was gathering for the spring campaign against the weakened, undermanned Confederate army. Realizing the Confederacy's urgent need to recruit more men for its armies, Cleburne cut boldly to the heart of the South's dilemma in one of the most remarkable documents of the Civil War. "We can see three great causes operating to destroy us," he argued. "First, the inferiority of our armies to those of the enemy in point of numbers; second, the poverty of our single source of supply [of manpower] in comparison with his several sources; third the fact that slavery, from being one of our chief sources of strength at the commencement of the war, has now become, in a military point of view, one of our chief sources of weakness." After cogently elaborating upon these three major points and presenting the various military, political, and diplomatic advantages that he believed could be derived from a drastic change in Confederate policy, Cleburne urged that the Confederacy should "immediately commence training a large reserve of the most courageous of our slaves, and further that we guarantee freedom within a reasonable time to every slave in the South who shall remain true to the Confederacy in this war."

Although Cleburne's proposal gained the endorsement of a dozen or so of his fellow officers, the commanding general, Joseph E. Johnston, refused to forward the document to Richmond on the grounds that "it was more political than military in tenor." Another high-ranking officer in the Army of Tennessee, however, was so indignant about the Cleburne proposal that he took it upon himself to forward a copy to President Davis. Upon receiving it, Davis ordered that the document be suppressed and that publicity about it be avoided. So successful was the suppression of Cleburne's remarkable proposal that its very existence did not become generally known until some thirty years after the war ended.

Davis probably felt that he had no alternative to suppression of the document, for there was one fatal weakness in Cleburne's otherwise brilliantly argued memorandum. The Confederate Constitution, so like the original United States Constitution in most ways, was distinctly unlike it in mentioning slavery explicitly at numerous points, in throwing safeguards around the basic principle that slavery in a sovereign state was exclusively the affair of that state, and in specifically barring Congress from passing any law "denying or impairing the right of property in negro slaves." How could Davis or any other mortal being convince eleven sovereign southern states, some of them headed by such near fanatics about states' rights as Governor Brown of Georgia and Governor Zebulon B. Vance of North Carolina, to abandon slavery? Davis might just as well have advised the sun not to rise or the tides of the ocean to cease.

Yet even as he ordered the suppression of Cleburne's proposal, Davis may well have been casting about in his mind for a less sweeping but more workable scheme for the freeing and arming of the slaves. He made carefully designed statements in the summer of 1864 that indicated his thinking about the South's ultimate purposes in the war. Vice President Stephens had declared in a famous speech in March 1861 that the Confederacy's "cornerstone rests upon the great truth, that the negro is not equal to the white man; that slavery—subordination to the superior race—is his natural and normal condition." As long as the United States refused to declare against slavery in the first year and a half of the war, Confederates had no pressing reason to examine and debate Stephens's "corner-stone" dogma and their own national priorities. But after January 1, 1863, and the changed policy of Lincoln and the North, the Confederates found themselves forced to confront painful realities and choices.

Jefferson Davis emerged as the foremost Confederate nationalist, and national independence became his consuming passion. In the summer of 1864 he gave a widely publicized interview in which he flatly declared, "We are not fighting for slavery. We are fighting for Independence, and that, or extermination, we *will* have." On a speaking tour through the Southeast following the fall of Atlanta in September 1864, Davis reiterated his emphasis on national independence as the supreme aim of the Confederacy. "Some there are," he confessed in an address at Augusta, Georgia, in October 1864, "who speak of reconstruction with slavery maintained; but are there any who would thus measure rights by property? God forbid."

Even before Davis could make his move as the would-be Confederate emancipator, a great public debate began throughout what was left of the Confederacy about the freeing and arming of the slaves. It was sparked by a proposal advanced by the *Richmond Enquirer*, which a historian has described as then "perhaps the finest daily newspaper in the South," one that commanded attention not only in the South but also in the North and in England, and one that generally supported the Davis administration. In October 1864 the *Enquirer* announced: "We should be glad to see the Confederate Congress provide for the purchase of two hundred and fifty thousand negroes, present them with their freedom and the privilege of remaining in the States, and arm, equip, drill and fight them." The *Enquirer's* proposal sparked a lively debate throughout much of the South, with a few newspapers and individuals endorsing the scheme and more vehemently opposing it. Prominent in the latter camp was the *North Carolina Standard* of William W. Holden, leader of the burgeoning peace movement in the Tar Heel state. Labeling the *Enquirer's* proposal "inexpressibly wrong" and calculated to demoralize the slaves while increasing the chances of the institution's destruction, Holden insisted that such an action by the Confederacy would demonstrate that "the white men of the Confederate States are not able to achieve their own liberties, and will thus in reality give up a contest which it will seek to prolong by the cowardly sacrifice of an unwarlike and comparatively innocent race." The *Charleston Mercury* likewise declared that the proposals were "as monstrous as they are insulting" and "treachery to our cause itself."

Given the furor caused by the Richmond newspaper's sugges-

tion, one can readily imagine the veritable storm of public controversy that greeted the plan for compensated, gradual emancipation proposed by President Davis in his message to Congress
of November 7, 1864. Modest in its immediate impact but far-
reaching—indeed revolutionary—in its implications, Davis's
plan called for the Confederate government, as a first step, to
purchase 40,000 adult male slaves; either to emancipate them
immediately or promise to emancipate them "after service faithfully rendered"; and to train them for noncombatant military
service. After thus making what he admitted was a "radical modification," Davis expressed his opposition, at least at that juncture,
to the idea of "a general levy and arming of the slaves for the duty
of soldiers." Should "the alternative ever be presented of subjugation or of the employment of the slave as a soldier," he added,
"there seems no reason to doubt what should then be our decision."

Though many historians later missed Davis's call for gradual,
compensated emancipation and the adroit finessing of the states'
control of slavery that he proposed, his contemporaries understood all too well what he was talking about and that he was
arguing that the matter of freeing the slaves should be dealt with
before the matter of arming them was taken up. For several
months Confederate newspapers engaged in what was probably
the most extensive, far-ranging debate concerning slavery that
the South had ever known. The brilliantly edited *Richmond Examiner*, one of the most influential critics of the Davis administration, cut to the heart of the matter when it assailed what it
regarded as the cardinal heresy in Davis's scheme: he assumed
that the blacks wished to be free and that freedom would be a
boon to them, an idea, the *Examiner* declared, which if the Southern people admitted as true "renders their position on the matter
of slavery utterly untenable." In a similar vein the *Richmond Whig*
suggested that if the slave had to fight "he should fight for the
blessings he enjoys as a slave, and not for the miseries that would
attend him if freed." That the *Charleston Mercury* anathematized
the Davis proposal surely surprised no one, but Davis and his
allies may well have been shocked by the extent and vehemence of

the editorial opposition. Even in far-away Texas, the *Galveston Tri-Weekly News* (refugeeing in Houston) deplored the proposal, as did the *Macon* (Georgia) *Telegraph and Confederate* and other papers.

Amidst all of the furor, there were a few newspapers that stood staunchly behind the president's plan. In North Carolina the *Wilmington Carolinian* not only supported it but went further: "We would have each State provide a homestead for the black soldier on his return home—*this as a reward*. And then we would give him freedom as a means of enjoying the property given him." The *Raleigh Confederate* also supported the Davis proposal and picked up this interesting passage from a speech made by Frederick Douglass in New York: "I am of [the] opinion that such is the confidence which the master can inspire over his slave, if Jeff. Davis goes about in earnest to raise a black army, making them suitable promises, they can be made very effective in the war for Southern independence. If Jeff. Davis will hold out to the blacks of the South their freedom—guarantee their freedom—the possession of a piece of land—the negroes of the South will fight, and fight valiantly for this boon."

Despite the opinion of Frederick Douglass, the nay-sayers both in the Confederate Congress and among southern newspapers had their way concerning Davis's proposal. Davis had loyal supporters in both houses of the Confederate Congress, but on his emancipation plan they were in a hopeless minority. Senators R.M.T. Hunter of Virginia, William A. Graham of North Carolina, and Louis T. Wigfall of Texas were three of the more prominent leaders of the opposition in the upper chamber, and Representative Henry S. Foote of Tennessee and other enemies of Davis had a field day in the House.

Perhaps the most hopeful development from Davis's viewpoint came when Governor William Smith of Virginia early in December 1864 urged the state legislature to face up to a painful question: "Is it indeed liberty and independence or subjugation which is presented to us? . . . For my part, standing before God and my country, I do not hesitate to say that I would arm such portion of our able-bodied slave population as may be necessary, and put them in the field . . . even if it resulted in the freedom of those thus organized." Smith, alone among southern governors save for Governor Henry W. Allen of Louisiana, thus lined up behind Davis. Perhaps it was the hope of eventual joint action by Virginia and the Confederate government that inspired Davis and Secretary of State Judah P. Benjamin to send Duncan F. Kenner to Britain and France early in 1865 as a secret envoy empowered to discuss Confederate emancipation, among other things, in exchange for Anglo-French recognition. The mission was abortive.

By early 1865 the Confederacy's military situation seemed well-nigh hopeless to many. General Sherman, having marched through Georgia and seized Savannah as a Christmas present for Lincoln, was poised for his march into the Carolinas. General Hood had led the Army of Tennessee into virtual annihilation in the battle of Nashville in mid-December. In Virginia, Lee held on tenaciously against Grant but had informed Davis early in November 1864 that "the inequality [in manpower] is too great." With war-weariness and despondency rising around him, Davis reluctantly agreed to send envoys to a so-called peace conference with Lincoln and Seward at Hampton Roads, Virginia, on February 3, 1865. Although Alexander Stephens, Senator Graham, William W. Holden, and numerous other prominent Confederates had clung to the belief that slavery might somehow be saved if the South agreed to end the war and return to the Union, they were in for a shock. Lincoln made it crystal clear at Hampton Roads that he and the federal government stood firmly by two great principles: the restoration of the Union and the abolition of slavery as envisioned in the Emancipation Proclamation and as soon to be constitutionally sanctioned by the proposed Thirteenth Amendment, which the United States Congress had just endorsed.

In the wake of the Hampton Roads conference, something like a Confederate revival occurred as great public meetings were held in Richmond and the remaining unconquered cities of the South. "There are no peace men among us now," declared the *Richmond Sentinel.* "There is no room for one; not an inch of ground for one to stand upon. We are all war men henceforth."

Calling for political measures to match the public mood, the *Sentinel* added: "Let our legislative bodies, *for mercy's* sake, now stop debate, and *act*."

The legislative bodies, both the Confederacy's and Virginia's, did finally act, but they took their sweet time about it and even then refrained from any mention of emancipation. The measure that the Confederate Congress ultimately approved on March 13, 1865, was introduced in the House on February 10 by one of Davis's staunchest supporters, Representative Ethelbert Barksdale of Mississippi. It provided for the arming of the slaves but specified that "nothing in the act shall be construed to authorize a change in the relation which the said slaves shall bear toward their owners." The passage of the bill was especially hard fought in the Senate, where it finally gained a one-vote margin only because the Virginia legislature instructed the state's two senators (one of whom, R.M.T. Hunter, was a leading opponent of the measure) to vote for it.

Perhaps the crucial factor in the enactment of even this limited measure for arming the slaves was the public intervention of Robert E. Lee. Chronically wary of becoming involved in politics, Lee had taken no public stand on President Davis's proposal in November 1864. Privately Lee had informed the chairman of the military affairs committee of the House of Representatives in late October or early November 1864 that he favored both the freeing and the arming of the slaves. That view was well known among political and military leaders, but the public only heard second-hand rumors of the charismatic general's views. "General Lee never speaks," a Charlottesville newspaper complained. ". . . . What does he think of our affairs? Should he speak, how the country would hang upon every word that fell from him!"

Lee finally did speak in mid-February 1865 in a letter to Barksdale that was, undoubtedly with Lee's consent, immediately made public. He strongly endorsed the Barksdale bill and argued that the Negroes would make efficient soldiers and that it would be "neither just nor wise, in my opinion, to require them to serve as slaves." Although the *Charleston Mercury* sneered that Lee had proven himself to be an apostle of "Southern Federalism and

Abolitionism," the *Richmond Sentinel* probably spoke for a much larger group, certainly in Virginia, when it announced that with "the great mass of our people, nothing more than [Lee's] letter is needed to settle every doubt or silence every objection."

Although both the Confederate law providing for the arming of the slaves and the complementary and necessary Virginia legislation skirted the question of emancipation, President Davis and the War Department bootlegged freedom into the plan when they promulgated the new policy. They did this by adding regulations, printed beneath the new Confederate law, with the fourth regulation stating that "No slave will be accepted as a recruit unless with his own consent and with the approbation of his master by a written instrument conferring, as far as he may, the rights of a freedman."

The new law was destined to have only a brief time in which to be tried, but scattered evidence revealed that there were some slaveholders willing to break with the past and smash the cornerstone—and also that there were blacks willing to become Confederate soldiers in exchange for freedom. Recruitment efforts were launched in various cities but went farthest in Richmond, where by late March 1865 Negroes in Confederate uniforms drilled and paraded. Time had run out for the Confederacy, however, and on April 9, 1865, Lee surrendered to Grant at Appomattox.

Davis, Lee, Benjamin, and a few other leaders had tried to bring the South to sacrifice one of its war aims, the preservation of slavery, in order to make a last great effort to achieve the other purpose, national independence. Even as southerners watched the Union reap rich advantages from Lincoln's policy of emancipating and recruiting the blacks, however, the Confederate Congress—and, one suspects, the majority of the southern people—demonstrated that even in the ultimate crisis they lacked the moral courage and imagination to begin voluntarily to abandon slavery.

The debate on the freeing and arming of the slaves was the fullest and freest discussion of slavery in which the South ever engaged, and it might have been a turning point in southern history. But the Confederate Congress first rejected President Davis's call for a change and then later, and too late, enacted an equivocal half-measure. The tragedy of the unturned corner was not in the military outcome of the war, for the North would probably have won in any event. But the history of Reconstruction and of long-term race relations in the South might well have been quite different if the Confederacy had embarked unequivocally on an emancipation policy. Where racial change was concerned, however, the majority of white southerners remained virtually unmovable—as the Reconstruction era would demonstrate in another and quite different set of circumstances.

❧

Reconstruction and Redemption
1865–1890

AT THE END of the Civil War the Confederates were a thoroughly beaten people. No die-hard guerrillas took to the Appalachians or to other refuges in an effort to continue resistance to the militarily triumphant forces of the Union. But passively accepting the military outcome of the war did not mean that white southerners suddenly repented of their past actions, for most did not. Slavery was dead, but in short order whites demonstrated their determination to maintain the subordination of the freed blacks, that is, to reestablish the supremacy of the white race by means other than the outright enslavement of the blacks.

Not only did the war's end leave the South impoverished and, in part, physically devastated, but most white southerners were embittered, confused, and spiritually exhausted. War and defeat proved to have no redeeming impact on the South's political life, either, for the defensive, narrow sectionalism that had warped and finally engulfed the South in the antebellum years reached new heights in the aftermath of the war. Indeed, as historian David Potter has persuasively argued, the "Civil War did far more to produce a southern nationalism which flourished in the cult of the Lost Cause than southern nationalism did to produce the war."

If the South's role in the postwar era known as Reconstruction was less far-sighted and constructive than it might have been, the same thing must, in fact, be said about the North's role. As Lincoln had realized better than most of the more radical Republicans, the strongest northern consensus was for the preservation of the Union. The North's secondary war aim of emancipating the slaves had been adopted cautiously and only under military and diplomatic pressure. Concerning the future status of the blacks in the United States, the best Lincoln could come up with when he broached the subject of emancipation in 1862 was to propose the voluntary colonization of the blacks outside the United States, possibly in Haiti or some other Caribbean land. Lincoln's abortive colonization proposals and projects were obviously designed in part to lessen the racist fears of white northerners who opposed or had misgivings about the emancipation policy. If most white southerners at the end of the war knew only or mainly that they wished to keep the blacks subordinate, most white northerners apparently did not know exactly what they wanted other than for slavery to be ended and for the freed blacks to stay out of the North. Reconstruction was doomed from the start to be a politically confused and troubled time.

As early as December 1863, Lincoln spelled out his plans—actually, his wartime hopes—for an easy, quick return of the South to full participation in the political life of the United States. He proposed a general amnesty and "restoration of all rights of property, except as to slaves," for all Confederates save a relatively few top civil and military officials, who would take an oath of present and future loyalty to the United States. Furthermore, whenever a nucleus of at least one-tenth of the 1860 voters in any southern state had taken such an oath, accepted the emancipation of the slaves, and formed a loyal (i.e., Unionist) state government, he would be willing to recognize such a government as the state's true one. Since the Constitution gave each branch of Congress the right to judge the qualifications of those elected to it, Lincoln could only hope that the Senate and House of Representatives would ultimately go along with his plans for a largely presidential Reconstruction.

In fact, Congress revealed clearly in 1864 that the majority of its members wanted a larger role in as well as a slower pace for the Reconstruction process. The strongly antislavery Radical Republicans struggled with and pushed Lincoln on a large number of matters. Although they were a minority even in their own party, on the matter of Reconstruction they gained sufficient support from others for Congress to pass the Wade-Davis Bill. Instead of Lincoln's 10 percent of the 1860 electorate, it would require 50 percent; and in lieu of the simple oath of loyalty that Lincoln would ask of ex-Confederates, it would require in addition an oath of past loyalty, that is, a statement that the oathtaker had never "voluntarily borne arms against the United States." The majority in Congress obviously felt no urgency about having the southern states fully restored, but the Wade-Davis Bill, like Lincoln's plan, made no provisions for blacks other than that slavery was to be ended.

Since Lincoln vetoed the Wade-Davis Bill and continued to push his own plan, the whole matter of Reconstruction was unsettled when the war ended. But Lincoln had given at first private and then, a few days before he was assassinated, public indications that he was modifying his views concerning the future of the blacks. If he was as astute a politician as most historians now believe he was—perhaps the nearest thing to a Gallup poll of northern public opinion that there was at the time—he probably believed that in response both to the valorous role of the blacks in the Union army and to other wartime events and experiences, the views of the northern white majority concerning the blacks had also changed, at least a little.

Lincoln tried to get Unionist state governments started in Arkansas, Virginia, Tennessee, and Louisiana. Although Congress accepted none of them, that in the federally controlled part of Louisiana was the farthest along. When Unionists there were about to draw up a new state constitution in the spring of 1864, Lincoln wrote the recently elected governor concerning the suffrage provision: "I barely suggest for your private consideration whether some of the colored people may not be let in [to vote] — as, for instance, the very intelligent and especially those who have fought gallantly in our ranks." The governor proved unable to persuade the Louisiana convention to follow Lincoln's advice, but on April 11, 1865, Lincoln addressed a crowd assembled at the White House to celebrate Lee's surrender. He devoted most of the speech to a defense of his approach to Reconstruction and particularly to his efforts to secure a loyal state government in Louisiana. For the first time Lincoln said publicly about black voting what he had earlier revealed only in private correspondence: "I would myself prefer that it [the vote] were now conferred on the very intelligent, and on those who serve our cause as soldiers." Pointing out that the new Louisiana constitution gave "the benefit of public schools equally to black and white" and at least empowered the legislature, if it wished, to give the vote to black men, Lincoln used a striking metaphor to defend his pragmatic approach: "Concede that the new government of Louisiana is only to what it should be as the egg is to the fowl, we shall sooner have the fowl by hatching the egg than by smashing it."

Lincoln's last speech was not, clearly, one of a colonizationist. He was saying, in effect, that American blacks not only were free but were in the United States to stay and that the doors of political and educational opportunity should be opened to them, perhaps gradually in the case of the vote but opened nonetheless. Unfortunately, too few white southerners heard or heeded the moderate recommendation, and in the furor surrounding Lincoln's assassination the whole nation lost sight of the speech.

While the debate and controversy about Reconstruction that went on in Washington throughout much of the war focused on the southern states, on the political future of Confederates, and, at the end of the war, on the status of the blacks, there were actually large national issues or stakes involved in Reconstruction and how it was to be carried out. Politically, the matter was of the utmost importance to both the Republican and the Democratic party. The Republicans, though championing the Union and American nationalism, were still at the end of the war what they had been at its beginning: an essentially sectional, all-northern political party. Their future in a fully restored Union, and one without the divisive issue of slavery, was problematical, to say the least. In advocating the generous and quick policy of restoring the southern states, Lincoln may well have been thinking in part of the large number of southern Whigs who had steadfastly refused to become Democrats and who might just be lured into a moderate Republican party now that slavery had been abolished.

The Republican party's dilemma at the end of the war was compounded by the fact that once the Thirteenth Amendment had forever abolished slavery, the South stood to gain additional political power. Instead of three-fifths of the slaves being counted for the purpose of apportioning representation in the House, all the blacks would be counted in the census of 1870—and the South would gain about twenty new congressmen and presidential electoral votes.

Some of the Radical Republicans, such as Senator Charles Sumner of Massachusetts, believed deeply that freedmen should receive the right to vote as a matter of principle. If they chose to vote for the party "that saved the Union and freed the slaves" and thus provided it with a southern wing, so much the better. In the entire North, however, only the New England states allowed black males equal access to the ballot box, and several northern states rejected moves to enfranchise blacks in 1865 and 1866. Sumner's preferred policy was therefore controversial even in the North and shunned by many Republicans, especially in the states of the Lower North.

If the Republicans were divided about the best way to handle the political aspects and impact of Reconstruction, the northern Democrats had no such problems. Though battered by the party's schism of 1860 and the subsequent secession and war, the Democracy survived in the North and had every reason to hope for the prompt restoration of the southern states and the return of the southern Democrats to the national party. While many northern Democrats had loyally supported the Unionist cause and fought in the federal army, others, especially in what was then the Midwest, had called for a negotiated peace in 1864 and bitterly criticized the Republican administration at every turn. Republicans labeled all northern Democrats "Copperheads," but that was a gross, partisan exaggeration.

One of the roots of midwestern Democratic opposition to the Republicans lay in the latter's economic policies. Partly as a result of wartime pressures and partly from Whiggish predilections, the Republicans during the war years raised the protective tariff to new heights, launched a new system of national banking, made lavish grants of public lands and generous loans of public money to private railway companies, and launched other policies that linked the federal government to the nation's economic life, particularly to its business and industrial sectors, in a neo-Hamiltonian, Whiggish fashion. The perpetuation of all these economic policies was, in fact, one of the key national stakes in Reconstruction, for the largely agrarian South, once fully participating again in the nation's political life, might well seek to alter the new dispensation.

In addition to the national political and economic stakes involved in Reconstruction, there was also a constitutional stake. Lincoln's bold use of executive power involved him in frequent clashes with Congress, though the exigencies of the war as well as his political finesse and flexibility helped contain or limit the conflict. Still, at the time of his death, Lincoln and the majority in Congress were stalemated on Reconstruction. The drive of some Republicans in Congress to check presidential power, a movement well under way during the war, was destined to accelerate in the early years of Reconstruction and, with the almost successful effort of the Republicans to oust President Andrew Johnson, came close to establishing the supremacy of Congress over the executive branch of the federal government.

Andrew Johnson, a lifelong Democrat from Tennessee and a staunch Unionist, had been chosen as Lincoln's running mate in 1864 simply because the Republicans wished to reincarnate themselves for the election as the Union party and woo as many votes among the War Democrats as possible. Despite strident language and an ancient hostility to the great planters of the South, Johnson's views and initial policies concerning Reconstruction turned out to be close to Lincoln's. Unlike Lincoln, however, Johnson had no reason to be concerned about the long-range future of the Republican party. Furthermore, where Lincoln was infinitely flexible when confronted with changing circumstances, Johnson tended to be rigid and dogmatic. One of his strengths was his profound faith in and respect for the Constitution. Yet that very strength ultimately became a weakness, for, in almost Calhounian fashion, Johnson clung to dogmas and niceties allegedly based on the constitution while ignoring great political and socioeconomic realities. Despite his passionate Unionism, Johnson turned out to be, in one sense, all too southern in his strict constitutionalism and sadly deficient as the intermediary and spokesman for the triumphant North in dealing with the vanquished South.

Acting while Congress was not in session, as Lincoln had done at the beginning of the war, Johnson in the summer of 1865 chose to proceed rapidly with Presidential Reconstruction and thus present Congress, when it did convene in December, with virtually an accomplished fact. His proclamation of amnesty and pardon for former Confederates was as generous and easy as Lincoln's policy had been, except that Johnson added to the excluded groups—those who had to make individual application to the president for pardon—all former Confederates who owned property worth $20,000 or more. Starting in North Carolina, Johnson named William W. Holden as provisional governor and authorized those Tar Heels who had earlier been eligible to vote and who took the loyalty oath to elect a convention that could reorganize the state government. Johnson further required of North Carolina and then the ten other ex-Confederate states that the ordinances of secession be nullified, the Thirteenth Amendment ratified, and the debts contracted as Confederate states repudiated.

The white southerners entrusted with carrying out Johnson's plans reacted variously. Some states hesitated over one aspect or another—the repudiation of state debts being an especially bitter pill for many in the creditor class—but ended up complying with the president's requirements. Mississippi, however, refused to ratify the Thirteenth Amendment, despite Johnson's urgings, yet the president ultimately accepted the state's new government. Alabama refused to ratify a portion of the amendment, and South Carolina repealed rather than nullified her ordinance of secession, thus implying that a quite legal action had simply been subsequently reversed. Both South Carolina and Mississippi refused to repudiate their Confederate debt. Such intransigent and defiant behavior on the part of some southern states late in 1865 began to make some northerners wonder if the white southerners truly acknowledged their defeat in the war.

On the important symbolic matter of black voting, Johnson, like Lincoln earlier, wrote letters to several of those he named as provisional governors advising and urging that the vote be given at least to educated or property-owning blacks. Johnson never demanded such a policy, however, and first Mississippi and then every other ex-Confederate state refused to make any concessions at all on the sensitive matter.

To the chagrin of some in the Upper South, where race relations were less strained, Mississippi led the way also in formulating new laws for the freedmen. Since the old slave codes were dead, new legislation was in fact necessary in order, among other things, to legalize and formalize black marriages and family ties. But in various ways—such as excluding blacks from jury service, restricting them to certain areas or occupations, prohibiting them from possessing firearms, and especially subjecting them to harsh vagrancy laws that could lead to long sentences of forced labor—Mississippi's "black code" and then those of most other southern states made all too clear that the Johnson-mandated state governments, representing the white southern majority, intended to establish a more or less permanent caste system that would keep blacks suspended in a half-way house between slavery and true freedom.

As if the black codes were not sufficient provocation to an increasingly aroused segment of the northern public, the voters in the South's special elections in the fall of 1865 selected a large number of prominent ex-Confederates to serve in Congress. Alexander Stephens, the former vice president of the Confederacy, was perhaps the most eminent of the group, but there were also several Confederate generals, a half-dozen Confederate cabinet officers, and fifty-eight men who had served in the Confederate Congress. A calm, dispassionate analyst might have noted that almost no fire-eating secessionists were elected and that, despite their positions in the Confederacy, many of those who were elected to office had been prewar Whigs and then Unionists as long as that had been possible under southern circumstances. As for Stephens, despite his Confederate office he had in reality opposed the Richmond government during most of the war and had probably helped significantly to weaken it. There were, however, few if any calm analysts in the immediate postwar years, for war hatreds and sectional passions still ran high in both North and South and would be many years in dying.

When Congress convened in December 1865, the Republican majority was even less in a mood to accept Presidential Reconstruction than it had been during Lincoln's time. Refusing to seat the newly elected senators and representatives from the South, the Republicans formed the Joint Committee on Reconstruction and prepared to seek a larger voice for Congress in the whole process of Reconstruction. United in their unwillingness to leave the matter solely in the president's hands and in their hostility to the black codes, the Republicans were, nevertheless, sharply divided as to what positive program to embrace. Sumner and a few others advocated a political revolution in the South that would guarantee for the blacks full citizenship, including the right to vote.

Representative Thaddeus Stevens of Pennsylvania, a powerful spokesman for the Radical Republicans, was less enthusiastic about enfranchising the blacks than about confiscating the land of ex-Confederates who owned 200 acres or more. He advocated parceling out a small portion of the seized land (an estimated 394 million acres) in forty-acre holdings to the freedmen and selling the great bulk of it to the highest bidder with the proceeds to be used to pay the United States' war debt, pensions to veterans of the Union army, and compensation to Unionists who had suffered property damages in the war. Although land was precisely what the great mass of southern blacks were most interested in, Stevens proved unable to sell his proposal even to his fellow Republicans. There were numerous reasons for that, including perhaps the Constitution's provision that, while Congress shall have the power to declare the punishment of treason, "no attainder of treason shall work corruption of blood, or forfeiture [of property] except during the life of the person attainted." But the Constitution proved to be quite amendable for other purposes in the era. In the last analysis, perhaps the main reason the freedmen got no land was the fact that their wishes and welfare were not the primary considerations of the dominant Republicans in Congress. As Stevens explained in another context, the Republicans' main mission was to find some way to guarantee the "perpetual ascendancy" of the party that claimed exclusive credit for having saved the Union.

The majority of the Republicans were, in fact, moderate in their views about Reconstruction, and many hoped to avoid an open clash with the president. In his dogmatic constitutionalism and unyielding defense of "his" southern state governments, however, Johnson shunned the opportunity to cooperate with the Republican majority. In March 1865, Lincoln had signed an act of Congress creating the Freedman's Bureau, which was designed primarily to assist the blacks in their transition to freedom but also to aid white Unionists in the South. Since the original bureau was established for only one year, the Republicans passed a measure early in 1866 extending its life and expanding its powers. Johnson vetoed the bill on the grounds that it gave the bureau military jurisdiction over certain cases involving freedmen even though civil courts were in operation in the southern states. Johnson's veto was at first narrowly upheld by Congress, but when he later vetoed a similar measure, the Republicans managed to override his opposition.

In response to the black codes, the Republicans in early 1866 also passed the Civil Rights Bill. It declared all persons born in the United States (except Indians not taxed) to be citizens and specified certain rights of citizens in addition to affirming that "such citizens of every race and color, without regard to any previous condition of slavery . . . shall have the same right, in every State and Territory . . . to full and equal benefit of all laws and proceedings for the security of person and property, as is enjoyed by white citizens." Arguing that the bill was unconstitutional, Johnson again used his veto power, only to have the Republicans again override him.

Congress too worried about the constitutionality of the Civil

Rights Act, however, for the substance of it was incorporated as the first section of an amendment to the Constitution, the Fourteenth, which the Republicans laboriously hammered together in the late spring of 1866. A compromise between the various Republican factions, the proposed amendment emerged as the terms of reunion acceptable to Congress. Moreover, the amendment served as a platform or program for Reconstruction with which Republicans could go into the congressional elections in the North in the fall of 1866. Those elections were crucial, for the Republicans needed larger majorities to be sure of the votes needed to override the president's vetoes.

In addition to the Fourteenth Amendment's first section, which gave federal protection to the civil rights and legal equality of all persons—thus forever prohibiting such state laws as the black codes—the amendment ingeniously handled the question of black voting, which was unpopular even in the North. It did this by forcing a painful choice upon the white southerners who controlled the Johnson-sponsored state governments: a state could enfranchise black adult males or not, as it wished, but if it denied the ballot to any adult male, "except for participation in rebellion" or other crime, then the state would have its basis of representation in Congress reduced in proportion to the number of persons disfranchised. This meant that the Fourteenth Amendment's voting section would protect not the blacks but the Republican party's control of the federal government.

The third section of the amendment struck at the South's traditional political leaders by barring from public office, state or federal, any person who had held public office before the war, had sworn to uphold the Constitution, and had then supported the Confederacy. The disqualification could be removed only by an act of Congress approved by a two-thirds majority. Finally, the fourth section upheld the validity of the United States' public debt while forever barring any payment of the Confederacy's debts.

Congress pointedly refrained from promising explicitly that ratification of the amendment by the southern states would be followed by their readmission to full and equal participation in the nation's government. Yet there was an implied promise, which many Republicans publicly declared they recognized, and when Tennessee, under the Republican leadership of Governor William G. Brownlow, ratified it, Congress readmitted the state and allowed its senators and representatives to be seated. The other ten ex-Confederate states, encouraged in their defiant recalcitrance by President Johnson, rejected the amendment and thus probably missed the best opportunity the South had to end Reconstruction without further rancor and turmoil. In the congressional elections in the North in November 1866, the Republicans won greater majorities than they had ever achieved and, since the South had rejected the essentially moderate terms offered in the Fourteenth Amendment, an angry Congress was in no mood for further temporizing.

The Military Reconstruction Acts of 1867, all passed over Johnson's vetoes, marked the beginning of a new phase known variously as Congressional or Radical or (by many white southerners) Black Reconstruction. The ten ex-Confederate states were divided into five military districts, each under the command of a general of the United States Army. These military governors were to conduct voter registration for which blacks would be eligible, while those ex-Confederates who were to be barred from officeholding under the proposed Fourteenth Amendment would be ineligible. This meant, in effect, that in five states of the Deep South, black voters were temporarily to outnumber white ones. Once the voter registration was completed, the states were to elect delegates to constitutional conventions, and these conventions were to write constitutions providing for universal manhood suffrage, meaning that blacks were to be enfranchised. When the new constitutions had been ratified by the voters and approved by Congress, and when the Fourteenth Amendment had been ratified, the states could regain their representation in Congress.

Many white southerners, especially those who now called themselves Conservatives in opposition to the Radicals, as all Republicans were called in the South, were traumatized by their fears of what might happen under Congressional Reconstruction. The mere fact of blacks voting, not to mention their composing the majority in five states, outraged the racial feelings of many whites. Yet in reality not only did Republican rule in the South, which was what Congressional Reconstruction actually meant, prove to be relatively short-lived in most states, but it was certainly not the orgy of corruption and misgovernment that Conservatives depicted and that became one of the longlived, potent myths of southern history.

As the Republicans in Congress trimmed the power of the Supreme Court and, after impeaching President Johnson, came within one vote of ousting him, Republican parties were organized in every southern state and undertook to write new state constitutions and take control of the state governments. The constitutions drawn up by the Republican-controlled conventions proved, on the whole, to be progressive improvements. They not only brought greater political democracy by providing for more equitable apportionment of legislatures and by making various offices elective rather than appointive, but they introduced reforms in various areas ranging from penal codes to the rights of women (not including, however, their right to vote). Perhaps the most important reform of all related to public schools, an area where most of the southern states had lagged in the antebellum era. The Republican constitutions committed the southern states, for the first time in some cases, to the broad principle of public support for schools. They were, except for a while in New Orleans, segregated according to race, and the actual education provided, as measured by such things as the length of the school term and expenditure per pupil, was pitifully inadequate by later standards. But at least an important foundation was laid and a beginning made.

Although blacks were the largest component of the Republican party in the South, they never held offices in proportion to their number as voters. The "Negro rule" or "Africanization" that Conservatives so passionately protested from the first was largely a figment of their imaginations. Except for the lower house in South Carolina, blacks were never in the majority in any southern legislature, and no black was ever elected as governor. Two blacks served as United States senators from Mississippi; fourteen blacks served in the House of Representatives; and a number of other blacks held state posts of varying importance. On the whole, the blacks who held these more prominent offices were educated, able men, some of them northern blacks who came to the South after the war, and some of them southern blacks.

The mass of blacks never got the land they so desperately wanted, and most were in the process of becoming impoverished sharecroppers as the political drama of Reconstruction unfolded. Yet the era was one of hopefulness, pride, and achievement for many blacks who took great satisfaction in participating in the democratic process and in seeing at least some members of their race elected to political office. In short, blacks did not rule during Congressional Reconstruction but they did play a significant role. That in itself was totally unacceptable to many southern whites.

There were native southern whites, however, who became Republicans and acquired from their opponents the unfortunate sobriquet of Scalawags. There were more of them in the Upper South than in the Deep South, and they were a richly varied lot. Many were former Whigs and some had been great slaveholding planters, such as James L. Alcorn of Mississippi and Daniel L. Russell, Jr., of North Carolina. Other Scalawags came from the ranks of yeoman farmers and either had been Unionists before the war or came during that ordeal to hold southern Democrats mainly responsible for it. While some Scalawags genuinely accepted the principle of civic or legal equality for their black allies, others merely went along opportunistically to make the best of what they regarded as a bad situation.

Just as the Scalawags defied simple categorization, so did the northern whites who moved South after the war, became Republicans when that party was born in the South in 1867–1868, and acquired the name Carpetbaggers. Some of them, such as Governor Adelbert Ames of Mississippi and Governor Daniel Chamberlain of South Carolina, were honest, able, and well-meaning men. Others were little more than political hacks if not crooks, and the postwar political scene—in the North as well as the South and certainly in the nation's capital—was one in which opportunities abounded for graft and shady dealing.

As soon as Republican rule began in the South, the Conservatives, who were essentially the southern Democrats but now with a large infusion of former Whigs, launched all-out political war. Virginia actually escaped Radical rule, for the Conservatives there successfully allied with moderate Republicans against the Radical faction, and by 1869 the Conservatives controlled the state. In that same year the Conservatives recaptured the government of Tennessee, and in 1870 they gained control of the legislature in North Carolina, where one of their first actions was to impeach and oust Republican Governor William W. Holden. In 1872 Georgia was "redeemed," as the Conservatives or Democrats liked to label their regaining of control, and by late 1876 Radical regimes survived only in South Carolina, Florida, and Louisiana.

Given all the advantages and the at least superficial strength which the Republicans seemed to have as Congressional Reconstruction began in 1867–1868, how were the Democrats able to regain control so quickly? The basic answer was quite simple. By enfranchising the blacks, first in the Military Reconstruction Acts and then, in 1869–1870, through the Fifteenth Amendment, which declared that the right of citizens to vote could not be abridged on account of race or color or "previous condition of servitude," the Republicans challenged at least the political dimension of white supremacy in the South. That challenge the majority of whites, whether planters or yeoman farmers or sharecroppers, found intolerable. When Democrats "drew the color line" and presented themselves as the white man's party locked in combat with the party of "Africanization" and "Negro rule," they had hit on a strategy that would prove incredibly successful for many decades to come. Virtually all historians agree now that the Democratic version of the situation was grossly inaccurate and oversimplified, but the fact remains that enough southern whites believed it then—and kept believing it for quite a while—that the South became what it had never before been: a region dominated by one political party, the Democrats. For about two decades, that is until the 1890s, there would be no sustained challenge to Democratic control in the South.

Along with the racist appeals that proved so potent, the Democrats, operating under the belief that their purpose of regaining control justified any means, resorted to intimidation and terrorism on a scale unprecedented in American experience. Left economically defenseless by the wholly political nature of Congressional Reconstruction, the blacks were especially vulnerable to economic pressure from white landowners and employers. If such tactics failed to work, the Democrats resorted to violence and terrorism aimed at white as well as black Republicans.

The best known of the terrorist organizations behind the Democratic drive to regain power in the South was the Ku Klux Klan. Begun in Tennessee, it became significant and powerful in various parts of the South as Congressional Reconstruction began in 1867. There were numerous secret organizations in addition to the Klan, but all of them sought to intimidate Republicans. If threats and scares did not accomplish that, then the organizations resorted to whippings, mutilation, and murder. Historian I.A. Newby aptly sums up the matter: "Altogether, the Redemption campaign involved the largest sustained application of violence and organized lawlessness in the peacetime history of the United States (unless one counts the campaign against the Indians as a peacetime operation)."

In addition to the Democrats' successful exploitation of white racism and the help they received from terrorists, there were other developments that weakened the Republicans. There was corruption in the Republican governments in the South; while it also existed on an even larger scale in other parts of the country at the time—and did not end after the Democrats took over—the fact remained that the issue helped the Democrats. Aside from the corruption, the Republicans increased the services rendered by the state government, as in the case of public schools, and that meant an increase in taxes. For impoverished people, as most southerners, white as well as black, were after the war, even modest taxes by later standards became a heavy burden. At one point in Mississippi, for example, one-fifth of the land in the state was put up for public sale because the owners had defaulted in their tax payments.

Southern Republicans increased their vulnerability by quarreling among themselves. The coalition of blacks, Scalawags, and Carpetbaggers was never an altogether easy one to maintain. A Tar Heel Republican rhapsodized during Reconstruction about "the royal oak of Republicanism—of which the Negro is the protecting bark, the white native the heart, the immigrant the vivifying sap." In reality, the so-called oak proved to be not so sturdy, as the two white groups watched each other suspiciously and both tried to persuade the blacks to deliver their votes without asking for anything like a commensurate share of the offices.

Republican rule in the South, weakened and challenged internally, also suffered as the North's commitment to the goals of Congressional Reconstruction waned. Except for the Radical Republicans, few northerners had ever been eager to see the blacks made legally equal and enfranchised citizens. Yet circumstances had led the Republicans to embrace that program as embodied in the Fourteenth and Fifteenth amendments. To enforce the amendments against the wishes of a hostile white majority in the South meant a larger, more consistent use of federal force than even many northern Republicans, not to mention Democrats, were willing to make. With the North's greatest hero of the Civil War, Ulysses S. Grant, as the winning presidential candidate of the Republicans in 1868 and again in 1872, the Democrats could hardly hope to wage a successful contest for that office. On other levels, however, especially in New York state and various states of the Lower North, the Democrats showed renewed vitality and increasingly bested the Republicans. The national Democratic party, favoring the acceptance of the new amendments to the Constitution as accomplished facts and the end of federal interference in the southern states—two policies almost contradictory—had rebounded sufficiently by 1874 to win a strong majority in the House of Representatives.

The final phase of Reconstruction in the South became entangled with the presidential election of 1876. In addition to northern weariness with what was called "the Southern question," the various scandals that besmirched the Grant administration and the economic depression that began in 1873 made the Democrats highly optimistic about their chances of victory. They named Governor Samuel J. Tilden of New York as their candidate, while the Republicans nominated Governor Rutherford B. Hayes of Ohio. Early returns showed Tilden to have carried most of the South plus several northern states and to have won a clear lead in the popular vote and 184 of the 185 electoral votes needed for victory. But Democratic victory celebrations proved premature, for confusion set in when both Democrats and Republicans claimed to have carried Florida, South Carolina, and Louisiana—the only states in the South still having Republican governments. The total number of electoral votes from those three states was nineteen; if Hayes could get them all, plus one technically disputed electoral vote from Oregon, then the Republicans would control the presidency for four more years.

The country faced a political crisis caused by uncertainty as to which candidate had won the election and by the strident claims of various spokesmen and politicians in both parties, each of which accused the other of trying to steal the election. Congress responded to the emergency by creating a fifteen-man Electoral Commission to investigate the returns from the disputed states and resolve the conflict. When the commission, composed of five members from each branch of Congress and five justices of the Supreme Court, ended up consisting of eight Republicans and seven Democrats and began to divide on strict party lines in its findings, the crisis entered a new stage. The Democrats controlled the House of Representatives, and many of them, especially those from the North, threatened to launch a filibuster or to do anything possible to prevent what they regarded as Tilden's being robbed of his victory.

As historian C. Vann Woodward first revealed, the southern Democrats, now returning to national political life in full force, struck a political bargain with the Hayes Republicans that resolved the crisis and settled the disputed election. Now known as the Compromise of 1877, the bargain had significant and long-range results for the South as well as the nation. The Republicans wanted the presidency, and the southern Democrats, now more concerned about dominating their own states and section than about playing a leading role in the nation's political life, wanted the last of the token federal troops withdrawn from the South and control of racial matters left in their own hands. Under the compromise, Hayes and the Republicans were to abandon federal efforts to protect the black Republicans in the South and leave compliance with the Fourteenth and Fifteenth amendments in the hands of the Redeemer Democrats. Hayes would receive all nineteen of the disputed electoral votes, and the Redeemers would certainly not join in any such "unpatriotic and imprudent" activity as a filibuster, but their party would take control of the state governments of South Carolina, Florida, and Louisiana.

The Redeemers wanted more, however, and the Hayes Republicans were willing to promise it. A Whiggish lot on the whole and, in fact, including a large number of prominent former Whigs, the southern Redeemers looked to railway development and industrialization as the great hope for the impoverished and still agrarian South. Would Hayes, himself a former Whig, be favorable to federal aid for a proposed Texas and Pacific railway and the myriad branch lines connected with it? Indeed he would, and that despite the federal scandals connected with such projects and policies during Grant's two terms.

There were other items on the agendas of both groups in the Compromise of 1877, and more recent scholars have argued that the negotiations described by Woodward were not actually decisive in the final outcome. Nevertheless, the basic fact for the South was that Reconstruction was finally ended and "the white man's party" was in firm control of the region. The psychic scars from the bitterness and violence of the era, most of it the result of the exaggerated fears and hatreds of southern whites themselves, would be long in healing. Bogged in economic deprivation partly caused by their own insistence upon white supremacy and black subordination, white southerners were also doomed to a long interlude of political parochialism and sectional defensiveness. Black southerners fared even worse, for the limited political gains they had made during Reconstruction were to be gradually eroded or diminished before being cancelled outright around the end of the century. The poorest of all in an economically stagnant, impoverished section, most blacks found their recently won freedom indeed a bare-bones affair.

In the closing years of the Reconstruction era some of the critics of the Redeemers began to call them Bourbon Democrats in the belief that, like the French royal line that was restored after Napoleon's defeat, they had neither learned nor forgotten anything from the Civil War. The name stuck, but it was misleading. The postwar leaders among the southern Democrats were by no means the same agrarian-minded planters who had dominated the party before the war, nor did they nostalgically hanker to restore the South to its antebellum form. Rather, the Redeemers were, on the whole, a business-oriented and Whiggish group who hoped to move the South into the mainstream of industrialization that was at the time transforming other portions of the United States into the world's leading industrial power. The South's actual achievements in industrialization were doomed to fall far short of the rhetorical goals and bright expectations. The fact remained, however, that the Redeemers envisioned a new South of factories, railways, and modern cities—a South in which upper- and middle-class whites would reap the most immediate benefits but one where, at least in theory, the great mass of impoverished whites and blacks would ultimately find jobs and reap material benefits. When the disparity between the glittering goals and the grim economic realities finally grew too painfully obvious, as happened in the 1890s, a full-scale political revolt confronted the southern Democrats.

In the 1870s and 1880s, however, the Redeemers ran the political show and shrewdly mixed their forward-looking economic programs with a veritable cult of the Lost Cause. Being a veteran of the Confederate army became a prime political asset for the ambitious southern politician. In Congress in 1876, for example, nine of the South's senators and forty-nine of its representatives were Confederate veterans. Two years later all of Alabama's eight seats in the House were filled by veterans, as were seven of Georgia's eight seats.

General John B. Gordon of Georgia well illustrates many

characteristics of the Redeemers. One of the ablest of the generals serving under Robert E. Lee, Gordon became a leading symbol of the Lost Cause when in 1889 he was elected as the first commander of the United Confederate Veterans. In addition to his ceremonial Confederate role, Gordon between the early 1870s and the late 1890s served two terms as governor and two terms in the United States Senate. He, Joseph E. Brown, and Alfred H. Colquitt made up Georgia's famed Bourbon triumvirate and for a full generation rotated among themselves the governorship and the two Senate seats. A lawyer who served for a time as counsel for one of the South's major railways, Gordon had investments in manufacturing, mining, and real estate as he held Georgia's highest political offices, advocated industrialization, and kept the Confederate tradition alive and potent.

With men such as Gordon prominent among the Democratic leadership in all the southern states, there were several salient policies that characterized the Redeemer regimes. Priding themselves on economy in government as a contrast to the alleged extravagance of the Republicans, the Democrats became almost obsessed with cutting public expenditures. Salaries of public officials, from the governors on down, were kept low, sometimes absurdly so, and various state services were either eliminated or severely cut. Perhaps public education at all levels was the greatest casualty, and the educational gap between the southern states and the rest of the nation grew wider after Reconstruction. Racial segregation required the expense of a dual school system, though the schools for blacks received nowhere near a fair share of support. In South Carolina, for example, blacks made up 61 percent of the school-age population in 1900 but their share of the school fund came to only 23 percent.

With public expenditures held down so drastically, taxes were understandably low. In Virginia, for example, the state collected in 1880 an average of $1.88 per capita. In view of the widespread and deep poverty, however, even low taxes were burdensome, and the agrarian majority grew to resent the fact that Redeemer tax policies favored business. With land as the principal object of taxation, the Democrats made generous tax concessions, such as ten-year exemptions from taxation, in order to attract railroads and new factories.

Concerning the blacks, the Redeemers were curiously ambivalent. On the one hand, to end Republican rule and restore "white supremacy"—that is, Democratic control—they were willing to go to great extremes either to prevent blacks from voting or to steal elections if necessary. On the other hand, at certain times and places some of the Redeemers, such as General Wade Hampton of South Carolina, managed to win some of the black votes for "the white man's party." Paternalistic in his racial attitude, Hampton and other Redeemer Democrats like him appointed some blacks to minor offices, supported token concessions to the blacks, and frowned on the rabid racism espoused by one wing of the Democratic party. Compared with those Democratic leaders who came after them, the Redeemers were actually racial moderates, not out of any belief in equalitarianism but through a strange mixture of paternalism and expediency.

Despite all the obstacles and the small chances for honest elections, blacks continued to vote even after the Compromise of 1877. One study suggests that in the presidential election of 1880 a majority of black men voted in nine southern states. The continuing fact of a significant number of black voters plus the survival of the Republican party, especially in the Upper South, meant that Democratic control in the last quarter of the century was far more precarious than it would be after 1900. The so-called "solid South" of the Democrats was, in fact, far from being solid and safe for that party. In 1890 a Mississippi Democrat made a frank confession that revealed facts applicable to much of the South: "It is no secret that there has not been a full vote and a fair count in Mississippi since 1875—that we have been preserving the ascendancy of the white people [i.e., the Democratic party] by revolutionary methods. In plain words, we have been stuffing ballot-boxes, committing perjury and here and there in the State carrying the elections by fraud and violence until the whole machinery for elections was about to rot down."

The truth was that one-party domination chafed and galled many southern whites, for historically the region was as much accustomed to political choice and two-party competition as any part of the country. The supremacy of whites had never actually been lost, even during Reconstruction, and after 1877 the real question was which class of whites would be supreme—the Redeemer businessmen-planters or the farmers, who constituted the vast agrarian majority. Scattered movements in opposition to the Redeemer Democrats and their policies began almost as soon as the Republican governments had been overthrown. Variously known as Independents or Insurgents, political leaders such as William H. Felton of Georgia, William M. Lowe of Alabama, and others challenged what they viewed as the Democratic oligarchy and won scattered successes. In Alabama a People's Anti-Bourbon party appeared in 1880, and the national Greenback party appeared in various parts of the South in the early 1880s.

The most sustained and successful challenge to the Democrats before the 1890s came in Virginia, where the Readjuster party led by General William Mahone gained control of the state for a few years. Virginia happened to be a special case, for in most of the southern states one of the top priorities for the Democrats upon regaining power was to reduce state debts and seek revenge for the repudiation of the Confederate debts that the Republicans had forced upon the South. Charging that the state debts incurred by the Republican-controlled governments were totally fraudulent, which was a complicated mixture of half-truth and exaggeration, the Democrats in the majority of southern states repudiated or reduced through scaling down over $100 million in state obligations.

Virginia, however, had never been under Radical control, and the Democrats were led by ultraconservatives who insisted that the state's honor and good name required the full payment of the debt, much of which had been incurred before the war. While the interest on the debt mounted in the depression-wracked 1870s, the Funders, as those who supported full payment of the debt were known, slashed government expenditures and services in order to meet the state's obligation to the bondholders. Finally the Funders diverted money earmarked for the state's newly established public schools and threatened to sabotage them alto-

gether if necessary. Revolt, long in building, came to a head in
1879, when those who wanted to scale down the debt formally
organized themselves as the Readjuster Party and waged a vigorous campaign that resulted in their gaining control of the legislature. A Richmond newspaper charged that the Readjusters
were preaching "communism of the worst sort," and while both
sides appealed for black votes, the Readjusters were the more
successful in winning them.

In 1880 the Readjusters elected their candidate to the governorship and finally succeeded in scaling down the debt. Much
more than the debt question was involved in the movement, however, for a larger purpose of the Readjusters, who represented an
alliance between the poorer white farmers and the blacks, was to
democratize Virginia's political life and have the government
serve more of the needs of the masses. The Readjusters repealed
the poll tax that the Democrats had enacted as a prerequisite for
voting, abolished the whipping post, shifted part of the tax load
off the farmers and onto railroads and other businesses, increased
state support for public schools, established a college for blacks,
chartered labor unions, and in general placed the Old Dominion
at the forefront of the southern states as far as reform and race
relations were concerned.

The reign of the Readjusters proved to be short-lived, however. Mahone, who went to the United States Senate in 1881 and
cast the deciding vote in favor of Republican organization of that
body, ruled the party in a controversial, high-handed fashion.
More basic in the overthrow of the Readjusters was the determination of the Virginia Democrats to "draw the color line" and do
whatever might be necessary, whether legal or not, to regain control, to "redeem" Virginia. Tactics developed earlier by southern
Democrats for use against Carpetbaggers and blacks were in 1883
used against fellow white Virginians. Championing white supremacy, the Democrats controlled the black vote when they
could or, when they could not, resorted to ballot-box stuffing and
other forms of chicanery. The climax of the bitter campaign came
when Democrats in Danville, Virginia, launched a bloody attack
on blacks that resulted in several deaths. "We have Virginia once

more in our possession," one Democratic spokesman boasted, "and we will keep her this time, be sure of that." One of the leading Funders later explained that the Democrats were "determined that they would never run the risk of falling under negro domination [!] again, and they accordingly amended the election laws so that the officers of election, if so inclined, could stuff the ballot boxes and cause them to make any returns that were desired."

In many ways, Virginia's Readjusters were a remarkable foreshadowing, aside from the particular issue of the state debt, of the southern Populists of the 1890s. But the Populist challenge to the stultifying one-party rule of the Democrats would be far more widespread throughout the South and more fundamental in its economic as well as political orientation. Moreover, the tactics whereby the Democrats eventually crushed the Populists—the appeal to white racism and exploitation of the myths of Reconstruction and its alleged black domination—were quite similar to those used by Virginia's Democrats in 1883.

Despite the many flaws and weaknesses of the Redeemer or Bourbon Democrats, they were by no means uniformly unscrupulous or hopeless. Their vision of an industrialized South, a vision too easy to dismiss as based on narrow class interests, was actually farsighted and wise. It was also a vision shared by many leaders of the dispossessed groups in the South, the farmers and the blacks. If the early twentieth century found the South still overwhelmingly agrarian, rural, and poor, the fact remains that the great majority of southerners looked to industrialization as the best hope for the future. The Redeemers helped to achieve that, and the important change of attitude or outlook was, as historian Carl Degler has argued, "the reconstruction that took." Congressional or Radical Reconstruction failed in its immediate political goals, but southerners voluntarily embraced the goal of industrialization and, in the long run, that more than any other single change would remake the South and lead in the twentieth century to its full reintegration into the mainstream of the nation's life. By 1890, however, as the Farmers' Alliance organized the impoverished and increasingly militant agrarian majority across the

South, that day of industrialization, and a general level of economic well-being that at least approached national norms, lay far in the future.

Rather than the optimism and nationalism of the Jeffersonian era, the South around 1890 was yet mired in sullen, defensive sectionalism and bitterly worsening relations between the races. Indeed, the transition from political leaders such as Jefferson himself, or Andrew Jackson or James Polk, to even the best of the Redeemer Democrats says much about the essentially tragic political fate of the South in the nineteenth century. That fate was no doubt affected by many developments, but surely a self-inflicted wound was the single greatest cause: the gradual surrender of the southern white majority, beginning in the 1820s, to the pride, fears, and hates of racism. Manifested before the Civil War in the white majority's fanatical defense of slavery as a positive good—a racial arrangement never to be changed—white racism after the war demanded a new kind of racial subordination for blacks through the black codes. They were outlawed by Congress, but the widespread intimidation of black voters during and after Reconstruction, the violent acts perpetrated against blacks, and the de facto segregation that long predated that which would ultimately be mandated by myriad laws in the South—all foreshadowed a new "peculiar institution" for the South, Jim Crow segregation, with its accompaniment of black disfranchisement. The South's greatest enemy in the nineteenth century, in short, proved all too sadly to be the great majority of southern whites.

Bibliographical Note

GENERAL

Given the challenging charge of surveying nineteenth-century southern politics down to the 1890s in a brief span, I have understandably had to pick and choose ruthlessly both in the narrative and in this highly selective bibliography. In light of the space limitation and the purpose of the volume, I have relied largely—but not exclusively—on secondary sources. Those that were most helpful or that offer newer and provocative interpretations are discussed below, even though in some cases among the latter group I do not find the arguments persuasive. For a more comprehensive listing of older works, the most convenient volume is *Writing Southern History: Essays in Historiography in Honor of Fletcher M. Green*, ed. Arthur S. Link and Rembert W. Patrick (Baton Rouge: Louisiana State Univ. Press, 1965).

Among general histories of the South, the newest is I.A. Newby, *The South: A History* (New York: Holt, Rinehart and Winston, 1978); while there is no bibliography the extensive footnotes are helpful. A slightly earlier volume is Monroe Lee Billington, *The American South: A Brief History* (New York: Scribner's, 1971). Older works made still useful by revision are Francis B. Simkins and Charles P. Roland, *A History of the South*, 4th ed. (New York: Knopf, 1972) and William B. Hesseltine and David L. Smiley, *The South in American History*, 2nd ed.(Englewood Cliffs, N.J.: Prentice-Hall, 1960). For the antebellum period alone, Clement Eaton's *A History of the Old South* (New York: Macmillan, 1949) is not as helpful as his *The Growth of Southern Civilization, 1790-1860* (New York: Harper and Row, 1961), which is in the New American Nation Series; and for the post-Civil War South, there is John S. Ezell, *The South since 1865* (New York: Macmillan, 1963).

Of the six volumes dealing altogether or in part with the nineteenth century in the distinguished series A History of the South, edited by Wendell H. Stephenson and E. Merton Coulter, the two most outstanding and still useful are Charles S. Sydnor, *The Development of Southern Sectionalism, 1819-1848* (Baton Rouge: Louisiana State Univ. Press, 1948) and C. Vann Woodward, *Origins of the New South, 1877-1913* (Baton Rouge: Louisiana State Univ. Press, 1951; with an updated bibliography by Charles B. Dew, 1971). As the work of one of this century's leading revisionist historians of the Civil War, Avery O. Craven's *The Growth of Southern Nationalism, 1848-1861* (Baton Rouge: Louisiana State Univ. Press, 1953) is important, and the Jeffersonian South is covered, albeit somewhat idiosyncratically, in Thomas P. Abernethy, *The South in the New Nation, 1789-1819* (Baton Rouge: Louisiana State Univ. Press, 1961). The two volumes by E. Merton Coulter, *The Confederate States of America, 1861-1865* (Baton Rouge: Louisiana State Univ. Press, 1950) and *The South During Reconstruction, 1865-1877* (Baton Rouge: Louisiana State Univ. Press, 1947) are not on a par with the others, especially the latter, in which the author's largely "un-Reconstructed" viewpoint warps both the interpretation and the coverage.

THE ERA OF THE VIRGINIA DYNASTY AND ANDREW JACKSON

For the South in the Jeffersonian era, in addition to the general works listed above, Marshall Smelser, *The Democratic Republic, 1801-1815* (New York: Harper and Row, 1968) offers a convenient overview and an extensive bibliography. More specifically focused on the politics of the period is Noble E. Cunningham, Jr., *The Jeffersonian Republicans in Power: Party Operations, 1801-1809* (Chapel Hill: Univ. of North Carolina Press, 1963) while Norman K. Risjord, *The Old Republicans: Southern Conservatism in the Age of Jefferson* (New York: Columbia Univ. Press, 1965) sheds much light on an important minority that foreshadowed later sectional themes and attitudes. James Broussard, *Southern Federalists, 1800-1816* (Baton Rouge: Louisiana State Univ. Press, 1978) skillfully traces the uphill battles of a declining minority.

The period between the War of 1812 and the election of Andrew Jackson is covered in George Dangerfield, *The Awakening of American Nationality, 1815-1828* (New York: Harper and Row, 1965); in the same New American Nation Series, Glyndon G. Van Deusen, *The Jacksonian Era* (New York: Harper and Brothers, 1959) is still useful. For the Compromise of 1820, Glover Moore, *The Missouri Controversy, 1819-1821* (Lexington: Univ. of Kentucky Press, 1953) is comprehensive; and the best book for the Nullification Crisis as well as for explaining the special circumstances of a crucially important state is William W. Freehling, *Prelude to Civil War: The Nullification Controversy in South Carolina, 1816-1836* (New York: Harper and Row, 1965).

THE SECOND PARTY SYSTEM

The second party system is the subject of some of the best southern political history in recent years. The system's origins across the nation are dealt with in Richard P. McCormick, *The Second American Party System: Party Formation in the Jacksonian Era* (Chapel Hill: Univ. of North Carolina Press, 1966). Two state studies, one in the Deep South and one in the Upper South, are illuminating for the entire region as well as useful for comparative purposes: J. Mills Thornton, III, *Politics and Power in a Slave Society: Alabama, 1800-1860* (Baton Rouge: Louisiana State Univ. Press, 1978) and Marc W. Kruman, *Parties and Politics in North Carolina, 1836-1865* (Baton Rouge: Louisiana State Univ. Press, 1983). William J. Cooper, Jr., *The South and the Politics of Slavery, 1828-1856* (Baton Rouge: Louisiana State Univ. Press, 1978) is focused, as the title suggests, on the single most enduringly important issue, while Robert Remini, *Andrew Jackson and the Bank War* (New York: W.W. Norton, 1967) deals with an economic issue of great national as well as state importance, especially in the 1830s and 1840s. The ideological differences between parties as well as sectional tensions are dealt with in Thomas B. Alexander, *Sectional Stress and Party Strength: A Computer Analysis of Roll-Call Voting Patterns in the United States House of Representatives, 1836-1860* (Nashville: Vanderbilt Univ. Press, 1967).

SECTIONALISM AND SECESSION

Despite the dubious emphasis on moral differences between North and South about slavery as the main source of sectional conflict, David Potter's *The Impending Crisis, 1848-1861* (New York: Harper and Row, 1976) is perhaps the most useful and penetrating study of the coming of the Civil War. It should be supplemented by Michael F. Holt, *The Political Crisis of the 1850s* (New York: John Wiley and Sons, 1978) and by two studies that share an influential but, in my judgment, incorrect interpretation of the southern states' reasons for seceding: Eugene Genovese, *The Political Economy of Slavery: Studies in the Economy and Society of the Old South* (New York: Vintage Books, 1967) and William L. Barney, *The Road to Secession: A New Perspective on the Old South* (New York: Praeger, 1972).

Important studies that go into more detail about various particular events or leaders than Potter has space for in his book are: Charles G. Sellers, *James K. Polk: Continentalist, 1843-1846* (Princeton: Princeton Univ. Press, 1966); Chaplain W. Morrison, *Democratic Politics and Sectionalism: The Wilmot Proviso Controversy* (Chapel Hill: Univ. of North Carolina Press, 1967); and Holman Hamilton, *Prologue to Conflict: The Crisis and Compromise of 1850* (New York: W.W. Norton, 1966). Democratizing constitutional changes in the southern states are treated in Fletcher M. Green, *Constitutional Development in the South Atlantic States, 1776-1860: A Study in the Evolution of Democracy* (Chapel Hill: Univ. of North Carolina Press, 1930) and more recently Ralph W. Wooster, *The People in Power: Courthouse and Statehouse in the Lower South* (Knoxville: Univ. of Tennessee Press, 1969) and *Politicians, Planters, and Plain Folk: Courthouse and Statehouse in the Upper South, 1850-1860* (Knoxville: Univ. of Tennessee Press, 1975).

The most detailed study of the leader who tried in vain to become the spokesman for the whole South is Charles M. Wiltse, *John C. Calhoun*, 3 vols. (Indianapolis: Bobbs-Merrill, 1944-1951), while the most readable biography is Margaret L. Coit, *John C. Calhoun: American Portrait* (Boston: Houghton Mifflin, 1950). The career of a key national figure in the 1850s who loomed large in southern political calculation and actions may best be studied in Robert W. Johannsen, *Stephen A. Douglas* (New York: Oxford Univ. Press, 1973). The portentous disintegration of the national organization of the Whig party is dealt with in the books mentioned above by Potter and Holt as well as in an older but still useful study by Arthur C. Cole, *The Whig Party in the South* (Washington: American Historical Association, 1913).

The secession crisis of 1860-1861 in the South has been a most puzzling—and controversial—subject for historians. While David M. Potter, *Lincoln and His Party in the Secession Crisis* (New Haven: Yale Univ. Press, 1942) is excellent, its limited focus is suggested by the title. Thornton's study of Alabama, mentioned above, is convincing in its emphasis on the democratic and white-libertarian impulse behind secession, while Steven Channing, *Crisis of Fear: Secession in South Carolina* (New York: Simon and Schuster, 1970) stresses the racial fears that gripped the white minority in that vanguard state. Two studies which reflect the influence of Eugene Genovese's dubious thesis about the hegemony of a slaveholding elite bent upon territorial expansion are William L. Barney, *The Secessionist Impulse: Alabama and Mississippi in 1860* (Princeton: Princeton Univ. Press, 1974) and Michael P. Johnson, *Toward a Patriarchal Republic: The Secession of Georgia* (Baton Rouge: Louisiana State Univ. Press, 1977). Michael Holt argues in the above-mentioned *The Political Crisis of the 1850s* that the presence of a continuing two-party system in the Upper South (unlike the Deep South in that decade) acted as a brake on extremism and delayed secession, but one wonders if he might not be interpreting a symptom as a cause. That is, the reason why a two-party system continued in the Upper South but not in the Deep South would seem to be more fundamental, and I suspect that the number of slaves, the overall demography, and the differing economies may have been significant in that respect.

THE CIVIL WAR

Although weak on the origins of secession, Emory M. Thomas, *The Confederate Nation, 1861-1865* (New York: Harper and Row, 1978) is now the best synthesis covering the South during the Civil War. A shorter, quite readable account but one without footnotes is Charles P. Roland, *The Confederacy* (Chicago: Univ. of Chicago Press, 1960). A long-time standby dealing with both North and South, especially useful for bibliographical purposes, James G. Randall and David H. Donald, *The Civil War and Reconstruction* (Boston: D.C. Heath, 1961), should now be supplemented by James M. McPherson, *Ordeal by Fire: The Civil War and Reconstruction* (New York: Knopf, 1982). More specifically dealing with the South, Thomas B. Alexander has advanced an influential thesis concerning "persistent Whiggery" and is coauthor, with Richard E. Beringer, of an important study of Confederate politics, *The Anatomy of the Confederate Congress: A Study of the Influences of Member Characteristics on Legislative Behavior, 1861-1865* (Nashville: Vanderbilt Univ. Press, 1972).

Although now outdated in some respects, Frank L. Owsley, *State Rights in the Confederacy* (Chicago: Univ. of Chicago Press, 1925) is still germane, as are two other older studies of internal dissent and problems: Albert B. Moore, *Conscription and Conflict in the Confederacy* (New York: Macmillan, 1924) and Georgia L. Tatum, *Disloyalty in the Confederacy* (Chapel Hill: Univ. of North Carolina Press, 1934). A more recent work that stresses popular disaffection and that faults the Confederacy's political leadership is Paul D. Escott, *After Secession: Jefferson Davis and the Failure of Confederate Nationalism* (Baton Rouge: Louisiana State Univ. Press, 1978). Frank E. Vandiver, on the other hand, is more sympathetic toward Davis's leadership in *Their Tattered Flags: The Epic of the Confederacy* (New York: Harper, 1970), and May S. Ringold, *The Role of State Legislatures in the Confederacy* (Athens: Univ. of Georgia Press, 1966) takes a more positive view of the southern state governments than does Owsley. Important antagonists of the Davis administration are the subjects of Richard E. Yates, *The Confederacy and Zeb Vance* (Tuscaloosa: Confederate Publishing Co., 1958) and Joseph H. Parks, *Joseph E. Brown of Georgia* (Baton Rouge: Louisiana State Univ. Press, 1977). Robert F. Durden, *The Gray and the Black: The Confederate Debate on Emancipation* (Baton Rouge: Louisiana State Univ. Press, 1972) deals with a significant political and military controversy within the Confederacy during the last year of its life; and relevant chapters, including especially one by Eric L. McKitrick, in William N. Chambers and Walter D. Burnham, eds., *The American Party Systems: Stages of Political Development* (New York: Oxford Univ. Press, 1967), are helpful.

THE RECONSTRUCTION ERA

For Reconstruction, the literature is much vaster than it is on the political aspects of the Confederacy; consequently, the titles that follow are highly selective. Convenient revisionist syntheses, in addition to those in the Randall-Donald and McPherson volumes (see above), may be found in Kenneth M. Stampp, *The Era of Reconstruction, 1865-1877* (New York: Vintage Books, 1965) and John Hope Franklin, *Reconstruction after the Civil War* (Chicago: Univ. of Chicago Press, 1961). The most recent account of Lincoln's approach to Reconstruction and the problem of racial adjustment is LaWanda Cox, *Lincoln and Black Freedom: A Study in Presidential Leadership* (Columbia: Univ. of South

Carolina Press, 1981), while Herman Belz, *Reconstructing the Union: Theory and Policy during the Civil War* (Ithaca: Cornell Univ. Press, 1969) and the same author's *Emancipation and Equal Rights: Politics and Constitutionalism in the Civil War Era* (New York: Norton, 1978) illuminate the Republican party's purposes and policies.

The long-dominant Beardian interpretation of Andrew Johnson and his battle with the Radical Republicans offered by Howard K. Beale, *The Critical Year: A Study of Andrew Johnson and Reconstruction* (New York: Frederick Ungar, 1930) has now been successfully challenged by a large number of newer studies. A few of the more important are: Eric L. McKitrick, *Andrew Johnson and Reconstruction* (Chicago: Univ. of Chicago Press, 1960); LaWanda Cox and John Cox, *Politics, Principle and Prejudice, 1865-1866: Dilemma of Reconstruction America* (New York: Free Press of Glencoe, 1963); W.R. Brock, *An American Crisis: Congress and Reconstruction, 1865-1867* (New York: St. Martin's, 1963); and Michael Les Benedict, *A Compromise of Principle: Congressional Republicans and Reconstruction, 1863-1869* (New York: W.W. Norton, 1974). The origins of two of the constitutional amendments of the Reconstruction era are analyzed in Joseph B. James, *The Framing of the Fourteenth Amendment* (Urbana: Univ. of Illinois Press, 1956) and William Gillette, *The Right to Vote: Politics and the Passage of the Fifteenth Amendment* (Baltimore: Johns Hopkins Univ. Press, 1965).

On the politics of the Southern states during Reconstruction the literature is too voluminous to be surveyed here, but convenient bibliographies may be found in the Randall-Donald and McPherson volumes (see above). Otto H. Olsen, ed., *The Reconstruction and Redemption of the South: An Assessment* (Baton Rouge: Louisiana State Univ. Press, 1980) is a good starting point for recent scholarship. On the role of the blacks in Reconstruction, Robert Cruden, *The Negro in Reconstruction* (Englewood Cliffs, N.J.: Prentice-Hall, 1969) is balanced and well suited for undergraduates; and two outstanding but more specialized studies are Joel Williamson, *After Slavery: The Negro in South Carolina during Reconstruction, 1861-1877* (Chapel Hill: Univ. of North Carolina Press, 1965) and Thomas Holt, *Black over White: Negro Political Leadership in South Carolina during Reconstruction*, (Urbana: Univ. of Illinois Press, 1977). The more recent and balanced view of the northerners who played prominent roles in the South's Republican parties is reflected in Richard N. Current, *Three Carpetbag*

Governors (Baton Rouge: Louisiana State Univ. Press, 1967); Otto H. Olsen, *Carpetbagger's Crusade: The Life of Albion W. Tourgee* (Baltimore: Johns Hopkins Univ. Press, 1965) is a reliable biography of a prominent figure in Reconstruction-era North Carolina. For the violent tactics that southern Democrats employed against the Republicans, white as well as black, the best study is Allen W. Trelease, *White Terror: The Ku Klux Klan Conspiracy and Southern Reconstruction* (New York: Harper and Row, 1971). The essays in J. Morgan Kousser and James M. McPherson, eds., *Region, Race, and Reconstruction: Essays in Honor of C. Vann Woodward* (New York: Oxford Univ. Press, 1982) are uniformly good, but two that are provocatively pertinent to Reconstruction are Lawrence N. Powell, "The Politics of Livelihood: Carpetbaggers in the Deep South," and J. Mills Thornton, III, "Fiscal Policy and the Failure of Radical Reconstruction in the Lower South."

Emphasizing the failure rather than the allegedly idealistic purposes of the Republicans' Reconstruction program, William Gillette, *Retreat from Reconstruction, 1869-1879* (Baton Rouge: Louisiana State Univ. Press, 1979) interweaves political developments in the South with those in Washington and the nation at large. The influential interpretation of the ending of Reconstruction advanced by C. Vann Woodward in *Reunion and Reaction: The Compromise of 1877 and the End of Reconstruction* (Boston: Little, Brown, 1951; rev. ed., 1956) has been unpersuasively challenged by, among others, Keith I. Polakoff, *The Politics of Inertia: The Election of 1876 and the End of Reconstruction* (Baton Rouge: Louisiana State Univ. Press, 1973).

Southern Democrats in the Saddle

Woodward's now classic portrait of the Redeemer Democrats in the above-mentioned *Origins of the New South* should be supplemented by Jack P. Maddex, *The Virginia Conservatives, 1867-1879: A Study in Reconstruction Politics* (Chapel Hill: Univ. of North Carolina Press, 1970); James Tice Moore, *Two Paths to the New South: The Virginia Debt Controversy, 1870-1883* (Lexington: Univ. Press of Kentucky, 1974); and William Cooper, *The Conservative Regime: South Carolina, 1877-1890* (Baltimore: Johns Hopkins Univ. Press, 1968). Eric Anderson, *Race and Politics in North Carolina, 1872-1901: The Black Second* (Baton Rouge: Louisiana State Univ. Press, 1981) focuses on one Tar Heel congressional district but sheds light on patterns and developments that were widespread across the South. The plight of southern

Republicans and the changing reactions thereto of the national party and its leaders are dealt with in Vincent P. De Santis, *Republicans Face the Southern Question: The New Departure Years, 1877-1897* (Baltimore: Johns Hopkins Univ. Press, 1959) and Stanley P. Hirshon, *Farewell to the Bloody Shirt: Northern Republicans and the Southern Negro, 1877-1893* (Chicago: Quadrangle Books, 1962). The various tactics employed by southern Democrats to disfranchise black voters as well as some white ones are analyzed in J. Morgan Kousser, *The Shaping of Southern Politics: Suffrage Restriction and the Establishment of the One-Party South, 1880-1910* (New Haven: Yale Univ. Press, 1974). Stopping short of the Populist Revolt of the 1890s, as does my own preceding narrative, Charles L. Flynn, Jr., in *White Land, Black Labor: Caste and Class in Late Nineteenth-Century Georgia* (Baton Rouge: Louisiana State Univ. Press, 1983), imaginatively integrates political and economic developments, as does also Steven Hahn, *The Roots of Southern Populism: Yeoman Farmers and the Transformation of the Georgia Upcountry, 1850-1890* (New York: Oxford Univ. Press, 1983).

Index

Adams, John Quincy, 34; foresees sectional party, 16–17; and 1824 election, 22–23, 26; opposes annexation of Texas, 48–49; on Mexican War, 52

"Africanization," 121

African slave trade: reopened by South Carolina, 31; divisive issue in 1850s, 78–79

Alabama, 80, 86, 87; gives white adult males the vote, 5; has democratic government, 41; and second-party system, 47; has early calls for Confederate change on slavery, 97; refuses to ratify part of Thirteenth Amendment, 113

Alcorn, James L., 97, 120

Alien and Sedition laws, 9

Allen, Henry W., 103

American Anti-Slavery Society, 44

American Colonization Society, 34

American Revolution, 1–2, 47

American System, 12, 21; as core of northern Whiggery, 45, 50

Ames, Adelbert, 120

"Anglo-Saxon" race, 40

Antietam (Sharpsburg), 94

antislavery movement: and Missouri crisis, 13–19; grows politically potent after 1846, 53–55; gains new impetus after 1854, 65–86

Appalachians, 107

Appomatox, 105

Arkansas, 17, 69, 80, 88, 95, 109; joins Union and has democratic government, 41; joins Confederacy, 90

Army of Tennessee, 98

Articles of Confederation, 2

Atchison, David, 66

Augusta, Georgia, 100

Baltimore, 5, 45, 80, 81

Baltimore Sun, 77

Bank of the United States, 11–12, 19–20, 28, 59

Baptists, 43

Barksdale, Ethelbert, 104

Beauregard, Pierre G.T., 90

Bell, John, 81–84

Benjamin, Judah P., 103

Benton, Thomas Hart, 20

Bible, 33

Biddle, Nicholas, 28

black belt, 45

blacks: in 1790 census, 2; accepted in Federal armed forces, 94; subject of Confederate debate, 96–104; recruited by Confederacy, 105; status as key question in Reconstruction, 107–11; subjected to harsh laws, 114; role during Congressional Reconstruction, 119–20; as target of Democrats'